Thomas Babington Macaulay

Lord Macaulay

The Task of the Modern Historian

Thomas Babington Macaulay

Lord Macaulay
The Task of the Modern Historian

ISBN/EAN: 9783337404246

Printed in Europe, USA, Canada, Australia, Japan

Cover: Foto ©ninafisch / pixelio.de

More available books at **www.hansebooks.com**

LITTLE MASTERPIECES

Little Masterpieces

Edited by Bliss Perry

LORD MACAULAY

THE TASK OF THE MODERN HISTORIAN

THE PURITANS

THE TRIAL OF WARREN HASTINGS

DR. SAMUEL JOHNSON

LORD BYRON

ENGLAND UNDER THE RESTORATION

THE DEATH OF CHARLES II.

THE RESTORATION OF 1688

THE ORIGIN OF THE NATIONAL DEBT

NEW YORK
DOUBLEDAY & McCLURE CO.
1898

Introduction

Editor's Introduction

This volume of selections from the writings of Macaulay begins with that portion of his essay on "History" which deals with the functions of the modern historian. It was written at the age of twenty-eight, and announced a program to which the author steadily conformed throughout his literary career. Three years before, Macaulay's essay on "Milton" had given him sudden fame, and the passage devoted to the Puritans, reprinted here, is a well-known example of the brilliant though somewhat over-accented style which was one of the causes of his immediate success with the public.

The pictorial method of writing history has never been more perfectly displayed than in the sketch of the trial of Warren Hastings. For fifty years it has been reprinted in reading-books; to use literally one of Macaulay's favorite and threadbare phrases, "every schoolboy" knows it; and yet it cannot be read without a thrill of enjoyment in the familiar scene, or without admiration for the author's workmanship.

Introduction

The essays devoted to Dr. Johnson and to Lord Byron reveal some of the limitations in sympathy and insight that are only too characteristic of Macaulay's mind. Dr. Johnson's gloomy spirit experienced passionate conflicts which the cheery, emphatic essayist could not comprehend ; nor was Macaulay altogether the man to measure the full sweep of Byron's wing. But the external traits of these two men of letters, and the impressions they made upon the London society of their times, are not likely to be so vividly depicted by any other hand. Nor has any critic pointed out more clearly than Macaulay certain defects— it is true they are very obvious defects—in Byron's dramatic poetry. The present volume gives only portions of the two essays, but the endeavor has been made to select those passages, which have the most permanent interest and value.

The first two extracts from the " History " are drawn from the famous third chapter, which surveys the state of England in 1685. Of those minute and racy depictions of the various aspects of English life at the Restoration ; the accounts of the country gentlemen and of the polite literature of the day are among the most skilful. The recital of the death of Charles II., at the opening of the fourth chap-

Introduction

ter, illustrates Macaulay's ease in narrative and his art in employing those insignificant details which the dignity of history has often neglected. The peculiar character of the Revolution of 1688, as it appeared to an English Whig at the middle of our own century, is next given, in a compact and admirable passage which closes the tenth chapter, of the "History." The selections end with a discussion, taken from the nineteenth chapter, of the origin of the national debt, in which Macaulay displays his wonted liveliness and his incurable political optimism.

Lord Macaulay suffers less than most writers of equal rank in being thus read by extracts. There is no league-long roll, either of thought or style, in the volumes with which he delighted his generation; the reader may venture upon his pages as upon a channel voyage of short chopping seas and bright breezy weather. He has been one of the most popular writers of the century; unfailingly entertaining, vigorous and clear, The time has indeed come, as Gladstone long ago predicted, when Macaulay is read with copious instruction but also with copious reserve. But whatever reserve the reader makes in view of Macaulay's obvious superficialities of thought and feeling, one cannot but respect his astounding infor-

Introduction

mation, his encouraging labor for the world's pleasure, and that honest, childlike admiration for his own age which made him confess, on entering the Crystal Palace exhibition of 1851, that he felt as he did on entering St. Peter's.

BLISS PERRY.

Contents

	PAGE
Editor's Introduction	vii

Essays—Selections.
    The Task of the Modern Historian......... 3
    The Puritans................................ 23
    The Trial of Warren Hastings............. 30
    Dr. Samuel Johnson....................... 43
        His Biographer........................ 43
        His Character and Career............. 52
    Lord Byron................................. 93
        The Man.............................. 93
        The Poet............................. 107

History of England—Selections.
    England under the Restoration............ 123
        The Country Gentlemen............... 123
        Polite Literature.................... 132
    The Death of Charles II.................. 146
    The Revolution of 1688................... 166
    The Origin of the National Debt.......... 180

Selected Essays

The Task of the Modern Historian

From the essay on History, *Edinburgh Review*
May, 1828.

THE best historians of later times have been seduced from truth, not by their imagination, but by their reason. They far excel their predecessors in the art of deducing general principles from facts. But, unhappily, they have fallen into the error of distorting facts to suit general principles. They arrive at the theory from looking at some of the phenomena, and the remaining phenomena they strain or curtail to suit the theory. For this purpose it is not necessary that they should assert what is absolutely false, for all questions in morals and politics are questions of comparison and degree. Any proposition which does not involve a contradiction in terms may, by possibility, be true; and if all the circumstances which raise a probability in its favor be stated and enforced, and those which lead to an opposite conclusion be omitted or lightly passed over, it may appear to be demonstrated. In every human char-

The Task of the Modern Historian

acter and transaction there is a mixture of good and evil;—a little exaggeration, a little suppression, a judicious use of epithets, a watchful and searching skepticism with respect to the evidence on one side, a convenient credulity with respect to every report or tradition on the other, may easily make a saint of Laud, or a tyrant of Henry the Fourth.

This species of misrepresentation abounds in the most valuable works of modern historians. Herodotus tells his story like a slovenly witness, who, heated by partialities and prejudices, unacquainted with the established rules of evidence, and uninstructed as to the obligations of his oath, confounds what he imagines with what he has seen and heard, and brings out facts, reports, conjectures, and fancies in one mass. Hume is an accomplished advocate. Without positively asserting much more than he can prove, he gives prominence to all the circumstances which support his case; he glides lightly over those which are unfavorable to it; his own witnesses are applauded and encouraged; the statements which seem to throw discredit on them are controverted; the contradictions into which they fall are explained away; a clear and connected abstract of their evidence is given. Every thing that is offered on the

The Task of the Modern Historian

other side is scrutinized with the utmost severity ; every suspicious circumstance is a ground for comment and invective ; what cannot be denied is extenuated, or passed by without notice ; concessions even are sometimes made ; but this insidious candor only increases the effect of the vast mass of sophistry.

We have mentioned Hume as the ablest and most popular writer of his class ; but the charge which we have brought against him is one to which all our most distinguished historians are in some degree obnoxious. Gibbon, in particular, deserves very severe censure. Of all the numerous culprits, however, none is more deeply guilty than Mr. Mitford. We willingly acknowledge the obligations which are due to his talents and industry. The modern historians of Greece had been in the habit of writing as if the world had learned nothing new during the last sixteen hundred years. Instead of illustrating the events which they narrated, by the philosophy of a more enlightened age, they judged of antiquity by itself alone. They seemed to think that notions, long driven from every other corner of literature, had a prescriptive right to occupy this last fastness. They considered all the ancient historians as equally authentic. They scarcely made any

The Task of the Modern Historian

distinction between him who related events at which he had himself been present, and him who, five hundred years after, composed a philosophical romance for a society which had, in the interval, undergone a complete change. It was all Greek, and all true! The centuries which separated Plutarch from Thucydides seemed as nothing to men who lived in an age so remote. The distance of time produced an error similar to that which is sometimes produced by distance of place. There are many good ladies who think that all the people in India live together, and who charge a friend setting out for Calcutta with kind messages to Bombay. To Rollin and Barthelemi, in the same manner, all the classics were contemporaries.

Mr. Mitford certainly introduced great improvements; he showed us that men who wrote in Greek and Latin sometimes told lies; he showed us that ancient history might be related in such a manner as to furnish not only allusions to schoolboys, but important lessons to statesmen. From that love of theatrical effect and high-flown sentiment which had poisoned almost every other work on the same subject, his book is perfectly free. But his passion for a theory as false, and far more ungenerous, led him substantially to

The Task of the Modern Historian

violate truth in every page. Sentiments unfavorable to democracy are made with unhesitating confidence, and with the utmost bitterness of language. Every charge brought against a monarch, or an aristocracy, is sifted with the utmost care. If it cannot be denied, some palliating supposition is suggested, or we are at least reminded that some circumstance now unknown *may* have justified what at present appears unjustifiable. Two events are reported by the same author in the same sentence ; their truth rests on the same testimony ; but the one supports the darling hypothesis, and the other seems inconsistent with it. The one is taken and the other is left.

The practice of distorting narrative into a conformity with theory, is a vice not so unfavorable as at first sight it may appear, to the interest of political science. We have compared the writers who indulge in it to advocates ; and we may add, that their conflicting fallacies, like those of advocates, correct each other. It has always been held, in the most enlightened nations, that a tribunal will decide a judicial question most fairly, when it has heard two able men argue, as unfairly as possible, on the two opposite sides of it ; and we are inclined to think that this

The Task of the Modern Historian

opinion is just. Sometimes, it is true, superior eloquence and dexterity will make the worse appear the better reason ; but it is at least certain that the judge will be compelled to contemplate the case under two different aspects. It is certain that no important consideration will altogether escape notice.

This is, at present, the state of history. The poet laureate appears for the Church of England, Lingard for the Church of Rome. Brodie has moved to set aside the verdicts obtained by Hume; and the cause in which Mitford succeeded is, we understand, about to be reheard. In the midst of these disputes, however, history proper, if we may use the term, is disappearing. The high, grave, impartial summing up of Thucydides is nowhere to be found.

While our historians are practising all the arts of controversy, they miserably neglect the art of narration, the art of interesting the affections and presenting pictures to the imagination. That a writer may produce these effects without violating truth, is sufficiently proved by many excellent biographical works. The immense popularity which well-written books of this kind have acquired, deserves the serious consideration of historians. Voltaire's Charles the Twelfth, Marmontel's Memoirs,

The Task of the Modern Historian

Boswell's Life of Johnson, Southey's Account of Nelson, are perused with delight by the most frivolous and indolent. Whenever any tolerable book of the same description makes its appearance, the circulating libraries are mobbed; the book societies are in commotion; the new novel lies uncut; the magazines and newspapers fill their columns with extracts. In the mean time, histories of great empires, written by men of eminent ability, lie unread on the shelves of ostentatious libraries.

The writers of history seem to entertain an aristocratical contempt for the writers of memoirs. They think it beneath the dignity of men who describe the revolutions of nations to dwell on the details which constitute the charm of biography. They have imposed on themselves a code of conventional decencies as absurd as that which has been the bane of the French drama. The most characteristic and interesting circumstances are omitted or softened down, because, as we are told, they are too trivial for the majesty of history. The majesty of history seems to resemble the majesty of the poor King of Spain, who died a martyr to ceremony, because the proper dignitaries were not at hand to render him assistance.

The Task of the Modern Historian

That history would be more amusing if this etiquette were relaxed, will, we suppose, be acknowledged. But would it be less dignified or useful? What do we mean, when we say that one past event is important, and another insignificant? No past event has any intrinsic importance. The knowledge of it is valuable only as it leads us to form just calculations with respect to the future. A history which does not serve this purpose, though it may be filled with battles, treaties, and commotions, is as useless as the series of turnpike-tickets collected by Sir Mathew Mite.

Let us suppose that Lord Clarendon, instead of filling hundreds of folio pages with copies of state-papers, in which the same assertions and contradictions are repeated, till the reader is overpowered with weariness, had condescended to be the Boswell of the Long Parliament. Let us suppose that he had exhibited to us the wise and lofty self-government of Hampden, leading while he seemed to follow, and propounding unanswerable arguments in the strongest forms, with the modest air of an inquirer anxious for information; the delusions which misled the noble spirit of Vane; the coarse fanaticism which concealed the yet loftier genius of Cromwell,

The Task of the Modern Historian

destined to control a mutinous army and a factious people, to abase the flag of Holland, to arrest the victorious arms of Sweden, and to hold the balance firm between the rival monarchies of France and Spain. Let us suppose that he had made his Cavaliers and Roundheads talk in their own style; that he had reported some of the ribaldry of Rupert's pages, and some of the cant of Harrison and Fleetwood. Would not his work, in that case, have been more interesting? Would it not have been more accurate?

A history in which every particular incident may be true, may on the whole be false. The circumstances which have most influence on the happiness of mankind, the changes of manners and morals, the transition of communities from poverty to wealth, from knowledge to ignorance, from ferocity to humanity—these are, for the most part, noiseless revolutions. Their progress is rarely indicated by what historians are pleased to call important events. They are not achieved by armies, or enacted by senates. They are sanctioned by no treaties, and recorded in no archives. They are carried on in every school, in every church, behind ten thousand counters, at ten thousand firesides. The upper current of society presents no

The Task of the Modern Historian

certain criterion by which we can judge of the direction in which the under current flows. We read of defeats and victories. But we know that nations may be miserable amidst victories, and prosperous amidst defeats. We read of the fall of wise ministers, and of the rise of profligate favorites. But we must remember how small a proportion the good or evil affected by a single statesman can bear to the good or evil of a great social system.

Bishop Watson compares a geologist to a gnat mounted on an elephant, and laying down theories as to the whole internal structure of the vast animal, from the phenomena of the hide. The comparison is unjust to the geologists; but it is very applicable to those historians who write as if the body politic were homogeneous, who look only on the surface of affairs, and never think of the mighty and various organization which lies deep below.

In the works of such writers as these, England, at the close of the Seven Years' War, is in the highest state of prosperity. At the close of the American War, she is in a miserable and degraded condition; as if the people were not on the whole as rich, as well governed, and as well educated at the latter period as at the former. We have read books

The Task of the Modern Historian

called Histories of England, under the reign of George the Second in which the rise of Methodism is not even mentioned. A hundred years hence, this breed of authors will, we hope, be extinct. If it should still exist, the late ministerial interregnum will be described in terms which will seem to imply that all government was at an end; that the social contract was annulled, and that the hand of every man was against his neighbor, until the wisdom and virtue of the new cabinet educed order out of the chaos of anarchy. We are quite certain that misconceptions as gross prevail at this moment, respecting many important parts of our annals.

The effect of historical reading is analogous, in many respects, to that produced by foreign travel. The student, like the tourist, is transported into a new state of society. He sees new fashions. He hears new modes of expression. His mind is enlarged by contemplating the wide diversities of laws, of morals, and of manners. But men may travel far, and return with minds as contracted as if they had never stirred from their own market-town. In the same manner, men may know the dates of many battles, and the genealogies of many royal houses, and yet be no wiser. Most people look at past times as

The Task of the Modern Historian

princes look at foreign countries. More than one illustrious stranger has landed on our island amidst the shouts of a mob, has dined with the king, has hunted with the master of the stag-hounds, has seen the guards reviewed, and a knight of the garter installed ; has cantered along Regent street ; has visited St. Paul's, and noted down its dimensions, and has then departed, thinking that he has seen England. He has, in fact, seen a few public buildings, public men, and public ceremonies. But of the vast and complex system of society, of the fine shades of national character, of the practical operation of government and laws, he knows nothing. He who would understand these things rightly, must not confine his observations to palaces and solemn days. He must see ordinary men as they appear in their ordinary business, and in their ordinary pleasures. He must mingle in the crowds of the exchange and the coffeehouse. He must obtain admittance to the convivial table and the domestic hearth. He must bear with vulgar expressions. He must not shrink from exploring even the retreats of misery. He who wishes to understand the condition of mankind in former ages, must proceed on the same principle. If he attends only to public transactions, to wars, con-

The Task of the Modern Historian

gresses, and debates, his studies will be as unprofitable as the travels of those imperial, royal, and serene sovereigns, who form their judgment of our island from having gone in state to a few fine sights, and from having held formal conferences with a few great officers.

✓The perfect historian is he in whose work the character and spirit of an age is exhibited in miniature. He relates no fact, he attributes no expression to his character, which is not authenticated by sufficient testimony. But by judicious selection, rejection, and arrangement, he gives to truth those attractions which have been usurped by fiction. In his narrative a due subordination is observed; some transactions are prominent, others retire. But the scale on which he represents them is increased or diminished, not according to the dignity of the persons concerned in them, but according to the degree in which they elucidate the condition of society and the nature of man. He shows us the court, the camp, and the senate. But he shows us also the nation. He considers no anecdote, no peculiarity of manner, no familiar saying, as too insignificant for his notice, which is not too insignificant to illustrate the operation of laws, of religion, and of education, and to mark the

The Task of the Modern Historian

progress of the human mind. Men will not merely be described, but will be made intimately known to us. The changes of manners will be indicated, not merely by a few general phrases, or a few extracts from statistical documents, but by appropriate images presented in every line.

If a man, such as we are supposing, should write the history of England, he would assuredly not omit the battles, the sieges, the negotiations, the seditions, the ministerial changes. But with these he would intersperse the details which are the charm of historical romances. At Lincoln Cathedral there is a beautiful painted window, which was made by an apprentice out of the pieces of glass which had been rejected by his master. It is so far superior to every other in the church, that, according to the tradition, the vanquished artist killed himself from mortification. Sir Walter Scott, in the same manner, has used those fragments of truth which historians have scornfully thrown behind them, in a manner which may well excite their envy. He has constructed out of their gleanings works which, even considered as histories, are scarcely less valuable than theirs. But a truly great historian would reclaim those materials which the novelist has appropriated.

The Task of the Modern Historian

The history of the government and the history of the people would be exhibited in that mode in which alone they can be exhibited justly, in inseparable conjunction and intermixture. We should not then have to look for the wars and votes of the Puritans in Clarendon, and for their phraseology in Old Mortality; for one half of King James in Hume, and for the other half in the Fortunes of Nigel.

The early part of our imaginary history would be rich with coloring from romance, ballad, and chronicle. We should find ourselves in the company of knights such as those of Froissart, and of pilgrims such as those who rode with Chaucer from the Tabard. Society would be shown from the highest to the lowest—from the royal cloth of state to the den of the outlaw; from the throne of the legate to the chimney-corner where the begging friar regaled himself. Palmers, minstrels, crusaders—the stately monastery, with the good cheer in its refectory, and the high-mass in its chapel—the manor-house, with its hunting and hawking—the tournament, with the heralds and ladies, the trumpets and the cloth of gold—would give truth and life to the representation. We should perceive, in a thousand slight touches, the importance of the privileged burgher,

The Task of the Modern Historian

and the fierce and haughty spirit which swelled under the collar of the degraded villain. The revival of letters would not merely be described in few magnificent periods. We should discern, in innumerable particulars, the fermentation of mind, the eager appetite for knowledge, which distinguished the sixteenth from the fifteenth century. In the Reformation we should see, not merely a schism which changed the ecclesiastical constitution of England and the mutual relations of the European powers, but a moral war which raged in every family, which set the father against the son, and the son against the father, the mother against the daughter, and the daughter against the mother. Henry would be painted with the skill of Tacitus. We should have the change of his character from his profuse and joyous youth to his savage and imperious old age. We should perceive the gradual progress of selfish and tyrannical passions, in a mind not naturally insensible or ungenerous ; and to the last we should detect some remains of that open and noble temper which endeared him to a people whom he oppressed, struggling with the hardness of despotism and the irritability of disease. We should see Elizabeth in all her weakness, and in all her strength, surrounded

The Task of the Modern Historian

by the handsome favorites whom she never trusted, and the wise old statesmen whom she never dismissed, uniting in herself the most contradictory qualities of both her parents—the coquetry, the caprice, the petty malice of Anne—the haughty and resolute spirit of Henry. We have no hesitation in saying, that a great artist might produce a portrait of this remarkable woman, at least as striking as that in the novel of Kenilworth, without employing a single trait not authenticated by ample testimony. In the mean time, we should see arts cultivated, wealth accumulated, the conveniences of life improved. We should see the keeps, where nobles, insecure themselves, spread insecurity around them, gradually giving place to the halls of peaceful opulence, to the oriels of Longleat, and the stately pinnacles of Burleigh. We should see towns extended, deserts cultivated, the hamlets of fishermen turned into wealthy havens, the meal of the peasant improved, and his hut more commodiously furnished. We should see those opinions and feelings which produced the great struggle against the house of Stuart, slowly growing up in the bosom of private families, before they manifested themselves in parliamentary debates. Then would come the civil war. Those

The Task of the Modern Historian

skirmishes, on which Clarendon dwells so minutely, would be told, as Thucydides would have told them, with perspicuous conciseness, They are merely connecting links. But the great characteristics of the age, the loyal enthusiasm of the brave English gentry, the fierce licentiousness of the swearing, dicing, drunken reprobates, whose excesses disgraced the royal cause—the austerity of the Presbyterian Sabbaths in the city, the extravagance of the Independent preachers in the camp, the precise garb, the severe countenance, the petty scruples, the affected accents, the absurd names and phrases which marked the Puritans—the valor, the policy, the public spirit which lurked beneath these ungraceful disguises—the dreams of the raving Fifth-monarchy-man—the dreams, scarcely less wild, of the philosophic republican—all these would enter into the representation, and render it at once more exact and more striking.

The instruction derived from history thus written would be of a vivid and practical character. It would be received by the imagination as well as by the reason. It would be not merely traced on the mind, but branded into it. Many truths, too, would be learned, which can be learned, in no other manner. As the history of states is generally written, the

The Task of the Modern Historian

greatest and most momentous revolutions seem to come upon them like supernatural inflictions, without warning or cause. But the fact is, that such revolutions are almost always the consequence of moral changes, which have gradually passed on the mass of the community, and which ordinarily proceed far before their progress is indicated by any public measure. An intimate knowledge of the domestic history of nations is therefore absolutely necessary to the prognosis of political events. A narrative defective in this respect is as useless as a medical treatise which should pass by all the symptoms attendant on the early stage of a disease, and mention only what occurs when the patient is beyond the reach of remedies.

An historian, such as we have been attempting to describe, would indeed be an intellectual prodigy. In his mind, powers, scarcely compatible with each other, must be tempered into an exquisite harmony. We shall sooner see another Shakspeare or another Homer. The highest excellence to which any single faculty can be brought would be less surprising than such a happy and delicate combination of qualities. Yet the contemplation of imaginary models is not an unpleasant or useless employment of the mind. It cannot

The Task of the Modern Historian

indeed produce perfection, but it produces improvement, and nourishes that generous and liberal fastidiousness, which is not inconsistent with the strongest sensibility to merit, and which, while it exalts our conceptions of the art, does not render us unjust to the artist.

The Puritans

From the essay on Milton, *Edinburgh Review,* August, 1825.

WE would speak first of the Puritans, the most remarkable body of men, perhaps, which the world has ever produced. The odious and ridiculous parts of their character lie on the surface. He that runs may read them ; nor have there been wanting attentive and malicious observers to point them out. For many years after the Restoration, they were the theme of unmeasured invective and derision. They were exposed to the utmost licentiousness of the press and of the stage, at the time when the press and the stage were most licentious. They were not men of letters ; they were, as a body, unpopular ; they could not defend themselves ; and the public would not take them under its protection. They were therefore abandoned, without reserve, to the tender mercies of the satirists and dramatists. The ostentatious simplicity of their dress, their sour aspect, their nasal twang, their stiff posture, their long graces, their Hebrew names, the Scrip-

The Puritans

tural phrases which they introduced on every occasion, their contempt of human learning, their detestation of polite amusements, were indeed fair game for the laughers. But it is not from the laughers alone that the philosophy of history is to be learnt. And he who approaches this subject should carefully guard against the influence of that potent ridicule, which has already misled so many excellent writers.

> " Ecco il fonte del riso, ed ecco il rio
> Che mortali perigli in se contiene:
> Hor qui tener a fren nostro a desio,
> Ed esser cauti molto a noi conviene."*

Those who roused the people to resistance —who directed their measures through a long series of eventful years—who formed, out of the most unpromising materials, the finest army that Europe had ever seen—who trampled down king, church, and aristocracy—who, in the short intervals of domestic sedition and rebellion, made the name of England terrible to every nation on the face of the earth, were no vulgar fanatics. Most of their absurdities were mere external badges, like the signs of freemasonry or the dresses of friars. We regret that these badges were not more attractive. We regret that a body, to whose courage and talents mankind has owed inesti-

* Gerusalemme Liberata, xv. 57.

The Puritans

mable obligations, had not the lofty elegance which distinguished some of the adherents of Charles I., or the easy good breeding for which the court of Charles II. was celebrated. But, if we must make our choice, we shall, like Bassanio in the play, turn from the specious caskets, which contain only the death's head and the fool's head, and fix our choice on the plain leaden chest which conceals the treasure.

The Puritans were men whose minds had derived a peculiar character from the daily contemplation of superior beings and external interests. Not content with acknowledging, in general terms, an overruling Providence, they habitually ascribed every event to the will of the Great Being, for whose power nothing was too vast, for whose inspection nothing was too minute. To know him, to serve him, to enjoy him, was with them the great end of existence. They rejected with contempt the ceremonious homage which other sects substituted for the pure worship of the soul. Instead of catching occasional glimpses of the Deity through an obscuring veil, they aspired to gaze full on the intolerable brightness, and to commune with him face to face. Hence originated their contempt for terrestrial distinctions. The difference between

The Puritans

the greatest and meanest of mankind seemed to vanish, when compared with the boundless interval which separated the whole race from him on whom their own eyes were constantly fixed. They recognized no title to superiority but his favor; and, confident of that favor, they despised all the accomplishments and all the dignities of the world. If they were unacquainted with the works of philosophers and poets, they were deeply read in the oracles of God. If their names were not found in the registers of heralds, they felt assured that they were recorded in the Book of Life. If their steps were not accompanied by a splendid train of menials, legions of ministering angels had charge over them. Their palaces were houses not made with hands: their diadems, crowns of glory which should never fade away! On the rich and the eloquent, on nobles and priests, they looked down with contempt: for they esteemed themselves rich in a more precious treasure, and eloquent in a more sublime language—nobles by the right of an earlier creation, and priests by the imposition of a mightier hand. The very meanest of them was a being to whose fate a mysterious and terrible importance belonged —on whose slightest actions the spirits of light and darkness looked with anxious interest

The Puritans

—who had been destined, before heaven and earth were created, to enjoy a felicity which should continue when heaven and earth should have passed away. Events which shortsighted politicians ascribed to earthly causes had been ordained on his account. For his sake empires had risen, and flourished, and decayed. For his sake the Almighty had proclaimed his will by the pen of the evangelist, and the harp of the prophet. He had been rescued by no common deliverer from the grasp of no common foe. He had been ransomed by the sweat of no vulgar agony, by the blood of no earthly sacrifice. It was for him that the sun had been darkened, that the rocks had been rent, that the dead had arisen, that all nature had shuddered at the sufferings of her expiring God!

Thus the Puritan was made up of two different men, the one all self-abasement, penitence, gratitude, passion ; the other proud, calm, inflexible, sagacious. He prostrated himself in the dust before his Maker ; but he set his foot on the neck of his king. In his devotional retirement, he prayed with convulsions, and groans, and tears. He was half maddened by glorious or terrible illusions. He heard the lyres of angels, or the tempting whispers of fiends. He caught a gleam of

The Puritans

the Beatific Vision, or woke screaming from the dreams of everlasting fire. Like Vane, he thought himself intrusted with the scepter of the millennial year. Like Fleetwood, he cried in the bitterness of his soul that God had hid his face from him. But when he took his seat in the council or girt on his sword for war, these tempestuous workings of the soul had left no perceptible trace behind them. People, who saw nothing of the godly but their uncouth visages, and heard nothing from them but their groans and their whining hymns, might laugh at them. But those had little reason to laugh who encountered them in the hall of debate, or in the field of battle. These fanatics brought to civil and military affairs a coolness of judgment and an immutability of purpose which some writers have thought inconsistent with their religious zeal, but which were in fact the necessary effects of it. The intensity of their feelings on one subject made them tranquil on every other. One overpowering sentiment had subjected to itself pity and hatred, ambition and fear. Death had lost its terrors and pleasure its charms. They had their smiles and their tears, their raptures and their sorrows, but not for the things of this world. Enthusiasm had made them Stoics,

The Puritans

had cleared their minds from every vulgar passion and prejudice, and raised them above the influence of danger and of corruption. It sometimes might lead them to pursue unwise ends, but never to choose unwise means. They went through the world like Sir Artegale's iron man Talus with his flail, crushing and trampling down oppressors, mingling with human beings, but having neither part nor lot in human infirmities; insensible to fatigue, to pleasure, and to pain, not to be pierced by any weapon, not to be withstood by any barrier,

Such we believe to have been the character of the Puritans. We perceive the absurdity of their manners. We dislike the sullen gloom of their domestic habits. We acknowledge that the tone of their minds was often injured by straining after things too high for mortal reach. And we know that, in spite of their hatred of Popery, they too often fell into the worst vices of that bad system, intolerance and extravagant austerity—that they had their anchorites and their crusades, their Dunstans and their De Montforts, their Dominics and their Escobars. Yet when all circumstances are taken into consideration, we do not hesitate to pronounce them a brave, a wise, an honest, and a useful body.

The Trial of Warren Hastings

From the essay on Warren Hastings, *Edinburgh Review*, October, 1841.

IN the mean time, the preparations for the trial had proceeded rapidly; and on the 13th of February, 1788, the sittings of the Court commenced. There have been spectacles more dazzling to the eye, more gorgeous with jewelry and cloth of gold, more attractive to grown-up children, than that which was then exhibited at Westminster; but, perhaps, there never was a spectacle so well calculated to strike a highly cultivated, a reflecting, an imaginative mind. All the various kinds of interest which belong to the near and to the distant, to the present and to the past, were collected on one spot and in one hour. All the talents and all the accomplishments which are developed by liberty and civilization were now displayed, with every advantage that could be derived both from co-operation and from contrast. Every step in the proceedings carried the mind either backward, through many troubled centuries, to the days when the

The Trial of Warren Hastings

foundations of the constitution were laid ; or far away, over boundless seas and deserts, to dusky nations living under strange stars, worshipping strange gods, and writing strange characters from right to left. The High Court of Parliament was to sit, according to forms handed down from the days of the Plantagenets, on an Englishman accused of exercising tyranny over the lord of the holy city of Benares, and the ladies of the princely house of Oude.

The place was worthy of such a trial. It was the great hall of William Rufus ; the hall which had resounded with acclamations at the inauguration of thirty kings ; the hall which had witnessed the just sentence of Bacon and the just absolution of Somers ; the hall where the eloquence of Strafford had for a moment awed and melted a victorious party inflamed with just resentment ; the hall where Charles had confronted the High Court of Justice with the placid courage which has half redeemed his fame. Neither military nor civil pomp was wanting. The avenues were lined with grenadiers. The streets were kept clear by cavalry. The peers, robed in gold and ermine, were marshalled by the heralds under Garter-King-at-Arms. The judges, in their vestments of state, attended to give advice on points of law.

The Trial of Warren Hastings

Near a hundred and seventy Lords, three-fourths of the Upper House, as the Upper House then was, walked in solemn order from their usual place of assembling to the tribunal. The junior baron present led the way— Lord Heathfield, recently ennobled for his memorable defence of Gibraltar against the fleets and armies of France and Spain. The long procession was closed by the Duke of Norfolk, Earl Marshal of the realm, by the great dignitaries, and by the brothers and sons of the king. Last of all came the Prince of Wales, conspicuous by his fine person and noble bearing. The gray old walls were hung with scarlet. The long galleries were crowded by such an audience as had rarely excited the fears or the emulation of an orator. There were gathered together, from all parts of a great, free, enlightened and prosperous realm, grace and female loveliness, wit and learning, the representatives of every science and of every art. There were seated around the queen the fair-haired young daughters of the house of Brunswick. There the ambassadors of great kings and commonwealths gazed with admiration on a spectacle which no other country in the world could present. There Siddons, in the prime of her majestic beauty, looked with emotion on a scene surpassing all the imi-

The Trial of Warren Hastings

tations of the stage. There the historian of the Roman Empire thought of the days when Cicero pleaded the cause of Sicily against Verres ; and when, before a senate which had still some show of freedom, Tacitus thundered against the oppressor of Africa. There were seen, side by side, the greatest painter and the greatest scholar of the age. The spectacle had allured Reynolds from that easel which has preserved to us the thoughtful foreheads of so many writers and statesmen, and the sweet smiles of so many noble matrons. It had induced Parr to suspend his labors in that dark and profound mine from which he had extracted a vast treasure of erudition —a treasure too often buried in the earth, too often paraded with injudicious and intelegant ostentation ; but still precious, massive, and splendid. There appeared the voluptuous charms of her to whom the heir of the throne had in secret plighted his faith. There, too, was she, the beautiful mother of a beautiful race, the Saint Cecilia, whose delicate features, lighted up by love and music, art has rescued from the common decay. There were the members of that brilliant society which quoted, criticised, and exchanged repartees, under the rich peacock hangings of Mrs. Montague. And here the

The Trial of Warren Hastings

ladies, whose lips, more persuasive than those of Fox himself, had carried the Westminster election against palace and treasury, shone round Georgiana Duchess of Devonshire.

The Sergeants made proclamation. Hastings advanced to the bar and bent his knee. The culprit was indeed not unworthy of that great presence. He had ruled an extensive and populous country, had made laws and treaties, had sent forth armies, had set up and pulled down princes. And in his high place he had so borne himself, that all had feared him, that most had loved him, and that hatred itself could deny him no title to glory, except virtue. He looked like a great man and not like a bad man. A person small and emaciated, yet deriving dignity from a carriage which, while it indicated deference to the court, indicated also habitual self-possession and self-respect ; a high and intellectual forehead ; a brow pensive, but not gloomy ; a mouth of inflexible decision ; a face pale and worn, but serene, on which was written, as legibly as under the great picture in the Council-chamber at Calcutta, *Mens æqua in arduis* ;— such was the aspect with which the great proconsul presented himself to his judges.

His counsel accompanied him, men all of whom were afterwards raised by their talents

The Trial of Warren Hastings

and learning to the highest posts in their profession—the bold and strong-minded Law, afterwards Chief Justice of the King's Bench; the more humane and eloquent Dallas, afterwards Chief Justice of the Common Pleas; and Plomer, who, nearly twenty years later, successfully conducted in the same high court the defence of Lord Melville, and subsequently became Vice-Chancellor and Master of the Rolls.

But neither the culprit nor his advocates attracted so much notice as the accusers. In the midst of the blaze of red drapery, a space had been fitted up with green benches and tables for the Commons. The managers, with Burke at their head, appeared in full dress. The collectors of gossip did not fail to remark that even Fox, generally so regardless of his appearance, had paid to the illustrious tribunal the compliment of wearing a bag and sword. Pitt had refused to be one of the conductors of the impeachment; and his commanding, copious, and sonorous eloquence was wanting to that great muster of various talents. Age and blindness had unfitted Lord North for the duties of a public prosecutor and his friends were left without the help of his excellent sense, his tact, and his urbanity But, in spite of the absence of these

The Trial of Warren Hastings

two distinguished members of the Lower House, the box in which the managers stood contained an array of speakers such as perhaps had not appeared together since the great age of Athenian eloquence. There stood Fox and Sheridan, the English Demosthenes and the English Hyperides. There was Burke, ignorant, indeed, or negligent of the art of adapting his reasonings and his style to the capacity and taste of his hearers; but in aptitude of comprehension and richness of imagination superior to every orator, ancient or modern. There, with eyes reverentially fixed on Burke, appeared the finest gentleman of the age—his form developed by every manly exercise—his face beaming with intelligence and spirit—the ingenious, the chivalrous, the high-souled Windham. Nor, though surrounded by such men, did the youngest manager pass unnoticed. At an age when most of those who distinguish themselves in life are still contending for prizes and fellowships at college, he had won for himself a conspicuous place in parliament. No advantage of fortune or connection was wanting that could set off to the height his splendid talents and his unblemished honor. At twenty-three he had been thought worthy to be ranked with the veteran statesmen who appeared as the delegates of the British Com-

The Trial of Warren Hastings

mons, at the bar of the British nobility. All who stood at that bar save him alone, are gone —culprit, advocates, accusers. To the generation which is now in the vigor of life, he is the sole representative of a great age which has passed away. But those who, within the last ten years, have listened with delight, till the morning sun shone on the tapestries of the House of Lords, to the lofty and animated eloquence of Charles Earl Grey, are able to form some estimate of the powers of a race of men among whom he was not the foremost.

The charges and the answers of Hastings were first read. This ceremony occupied two whole days, and was rendered less tedious than it would otherwise have been, by the silver voice and just emphasis of Cowper, the clerk of the court, a near relation of the amiable poet. On the third day Burke rose. Four sittings of the court were occupied by his opening speech, which was intended to be a general introduction to all the charges. With an exuberance of thought and a splendor of diction which more than satisfied the highly-raised expectation of the audience, he described the character and institutions of the natives of India ; recounted the circumstances in which the Asiatic empire of Britain had originated ; and set forth the constitution of

The Trial of Warren Hastings

the Company and of the English Presidencies. Having thus attempted to communicate to his hearers an idea of Eastern society, as vivid as that which existed in his own mind, he proceeded to arrange the administration of Hastings, as systematically conducted in defiance of morality and public law. The energy and pathos of the great orator extorted expressions of unwonted admiration even from the stern and hostile Chancellor; and for a moment, seemed to pierce even the resolute heart of the defendant. The ladies in the galleries, unaccustomed to such displays of eloquence, excited by the solemnity of the occasion, and perhaps not unwilling to display their taste and sensibility, were in a state of uncontrollable emotion. Handkerchiefs were pulled out; smelling bottles were handed round; hysterical sobs and screams were heard; and Mrs. Sheridan was carried out in a fit. At length the orator concluded. Raising his voice till the old arches of Irish oak resounded—"Therefore," said he, "hath it with all confidence been ordered by the Commons of Great Britain, that I impeach Warren Hastings of high crimes and misdemeanors. I impeach him in the name of the Commons House of Parliament, whose trust he has betrayed. I impeach him in the name of the

The Trial of Warren Hastings

English nation, whose ancient honor he has sullied. I impeach him in the name of the people of India, whose rights he has trodden under foot, and whose country he has turned into a desert. Lastly, in the name of human nature itself, in the name of both sexes, in the name of every age, in the name of every rank, I impeach the common enemy and oppressor of all!"

When the deep murmur of various emotions had subsided, Mr. Fox rose to address the Lords respecting the course of proceedings to be followed. The wish of the accuser was, that the court would bring to a close the investigation of the first charge before the second was opened. The wish of Hastings and his counsel was, that the managers should open all the charges, and produce all the evidence for the prosecution, before the defence began. The Lords retired to their own house, to consider the question. The Chancellor took the side of Hastings. Lord Loughborough, who was now in opposition, supported the demand of the managers. The division showed which way the inclination of the tribunal leaned. A majority of near three to one decided in favor of the course for which Hastings contended.

When the court sat again, Mr. Fox, assisted

The Trial of Warren Hastings

by Mr. Grey, opened the charge respecting Cheyte Sing, and several days were spent in reading papers and hearing witnesses. The next article was that relating to the Princesses of Oude. The conduct of this part of the case was intrusted to Sheridan. The curiosity of the public to hear him was unbounded. The sparkling and highly-finished declamation lasted two days; but the Hall was crowded to suffocation during the whole time. It was said that fifty guineas had been paid for a single ticket. Sheridan, when he concluded, contrived, with a knowledge of stage-effect which his father might have envied, to sink back, as if exhausted, into the arms of Burke, who hugged him with the energy of generous admiration!

June was now far advanced. The session could not last much longer, and the progress which had been made in the impeachment was not very satisfactory. There were twenty charges. On two only of these had even the case for the prosecution been heard; and it was now a year since Hastings had been admitted to bail.

The interest taken by the public in the trial was great when the court began to sit, and rose to the height when Sheridan spoke on the charges relating to the Begums. From that time the excitement went down fast. The

The Trial of Warren Hastings

spectacle had lost the attraction of novelty. The great displays of rhetoric were over. What was behind was not of a nature to entice men of letters from their books in the morning, or to tempt ladies who had left the masquerade at two, to be out of bed before eight. There remained examinations and cross-examinations. There remained statements of accounts. There remained the reading of papers, filled with words unintelligible to English ears—with lacs and crores, zemindars and aumils, sunnuds and perwannahs, jagnires and nuzzurs. There remained bickerings, not always carried on with the best taste or with the best temper, between the managers of the impeachment and the counsel for the defence, particularly between Mr. Burke and Mr. Law. There remained the endless marches and countermarches of the Peers between their house and the hall; for as often as a point of law was to be discussed their lordships retired to discuss it apart; and the consequence was, as the late Lord Stanhope wittily said, that the judges walked and the trial stood still.

It is to be added, that in the spring of 1788, when the trial commenced, no important question, either of domestic or foreign policy, excited the public mind. The proceeding in Westminster Hall, therefore naturally ex-

The Trial of Warren Hastings

cited most of the attention of Parliament and of the public. It was the one great event of that season. But in the following year, the king's illness, the debates on the regency, the expectation of a change of ministry, completely diverted public attention from Indian affairs ; and within a fortnight after George the Third had returned thanks in St. Paul's for his recovery, the States General of France met at Versailles. In the midst of the agitation produced by those events, the impeachment was for a time almost forgotten.

Dr. Samuel Johnson

From the essay on Croker's Edition of Boswell's Life of Johnson, *Edinburgh Review*, September 1831.

His Biographer

The Life of Johnson is assuredly a great, a very great work. Homer is not more decidedly the first of heroic poets, Shakspeare is not more decidedly the first of dramatists, Demosthenes is not more decidedly the first of orators, than Boswell is the first of biographers. He has no second. He has distanced all his competitors so decidedly, that it is not worth while to place them. Eclipse is first, and the rest nowhere.

We are not sure that there is in the whole history of the human intellect so strange a phenomenon as this book. Many of the greatest men that ever lived have written biography. Boswell was one of the smallest men that ever lived; and he has beaten them all. He was, if we are to give any credit to his own account, or to the united testimony of all who knew him, a man of the meanest

Dr. Samuel Johnson

and feeblest intellect. Johnson described him as a fellow who had missed his only chance of immortality, by not having been alive when the Dunciad was written. Beauclerk used his name as a proverbial expression for a bore. He was the laughing-stock of the whole of that brilliant society which has owed to him the greater part of its fame. He was always laying himself at the feet of some eminent man, and begging to be spit upon and trampled upon. He was always earning some ridiculous nickname, and then, "binding it as a crown unto him,"—not merely in metaphor, but literally. He exhibited himself at the Shakspeare Jubilee, to all the crowd which filled Stratford-on-Avon, with a placard around his hat bearing the inscription of *Corsica Boswell*. In his Tour, he proclaimed to all the world, that at Edinburgh he was known by the appellation of *Paoli Boswell*. Servile and impertinent—shallow and pedantic—a bigot and a sot—bloated with family pride, and eternally blustering about the dignity of a born gentleman, yet stooping to be a talebearer, an eavesdropper, a common butt in the taverns of London—so curious to know everybody who was talked about, that Tory and High Churchman as he was, he maneuvered, we have been told, for

Dr. Samuel Johnson

an introduction to Tom Paine—so vain of the most childish distinctions, that, when he had been to court, he drove to the office where his book was being printed without changing his clothes, and summoned all the printer's devils to admire his new ruffles and sword; such was this man; and such he was content and proud to be. Everything which another man would have hidden—everything, the publication of which would have made another man hang himself, was matter of gay and clamorous exultation to his weak and diseased mind. What silly things he said—what bitter retorts he provoked—how at one place he was troubled with evil presentiments which came to nothing—how at another place, on waking from a drunken doze, he read the Prayer-book, and took a hair of the dog that had bitten him—how he went to see men hanged, and came away maudlin—how he added five hundred pounds to the fortune of one of his babies, because she was not frightened at Johnson's ugly face—how he was frightened out of his wits at sea—and how the sailors quieted him as they would have quieted a child—how tipsy he was at Lady Cork's one evening, and how much his merriment annoyed the ladies—how impertinent he was to the Duchess of Argyle, and

Dr. Samuel Johnson

with what stately contempt she put down his impertinence—how Colonel Macleod sneered to his face at his impudent obtrusiveness—how his father and the very wife of his bosom laughed and fretted at his fooleries—all these things he proclaimed to all the world, as if they had been subjects for pride and ostentatious rejoicing. All the caprices of his temper, all the illusions of his vanity, all the hypochondriac whimsies, all his castles in the air, he displayed with a cool self-complacency, a perfect unconsciousness that he was making a fool of himself, to which it is impossible to find a parallel in the whole history of mankind. He has used many people ill, but assuredly he has used nobody so ill as himself.

That such a man should have written one of the best books in the world, is strange enough. But this is not all. Many persons who have conducted themselves foolishly in active life, and whose conversation has indicated no superior powers of mind, have written valuable books. Goldsmith was very justly described by one of his contemporaries as an inspired idiot, and by another as a being,

"Who wrote like an angel, and talked like poor Poll."

La Fontaine was in society a mere simpleton.

Dr. Samuel Johnson

His blunders would not come in amiss among the stories of Hierocles. But these men attained literary eminence in spite of their weaknesses. Boswell attained it by reason of his weaknesses. If he had not been a great fool, he would never have been a great writer. Without all the qualities which made him the jest and the torment of those among whom he lived—without the officiousness, the inquisitiveness, the effrontery, the toad-eating, the insensibility to all reproof, he never could have produced so excellent a book. He was a slave, proud of his servitude : a Paul Pry, convinced that his own curiosity and garrulity were virtues ; an unsafe companion, who never scrupled to repay the most liberal hospitality by the basest violation of confidence ; a man without delicacy, without shame, without sense enough to know when he was hurting the feelings of others, or when he was exposing himself to derision ; and because he was all this, he has, in an important department of literature, immeasurably surpassed such writers as Tacitus, Clarendon, Alfieri, and his own idol Johnson.

Of the talents which ordinarily raise men to eminence as writers, he had absolutely none. There is not, in all his books, a single remark of his own on literature, politics, re-

Dr. Samuel Johnson

ligion, or society, which is not either commonplace or absurd. His dissertations on hereditary gentility, on the slave trade, and on the entailing of landed estates, may serve as examples. To say that these passages are sophistical, would be to pay them an extravagant compliment. They have no pretense to argument or even to meaning. He has reported innumerable observations made by himself in the course of conversation. Of those observations we do not remember one which is above the intellectual capacity of a boy of fifteen. He has printed many of his own letters, and in these letters he is always ranting or twaddling. Logic, eloquence, wit, taste, all those things which are generally considered as making a book valuable, were utterly wanting to him. He had, indeed, a quick observation and a retentive memory. These qualities, if he had been a man of sense and virtue, would scarcely of themselves have sufficed to make him conspicuous; but, as he was a dunce, a parasite, and a coxcomb, they have made him immortal.

Those parts of his book which, considered abstractedly, are most utterly worthless, are delightful when we read them as illustrations of the character of the writer. Bad in themselves, they are good dramatically, like the

Dr. Samuel Johnson

nonsense of Justice Shallow, the clipped English of Dr. Caius, or the misplaced consonants of Fluellen. Of all confessors, Boswell is the most candid. Other men who have pretended to lay open their own hearts—Rousseau, for example, and Lord Byron—have evidently written with a constant view to effect, and are to be then most distrusted when they seem to be most sincere. There is scarcely any man who would not rather accuse himself of great crimes and of dark and tempestuous passions, than proclaim all his little vanities, and all his wild fancies. It would be easier to find a person who would avow actions like those of Cæsar Borgia or Danton, than one who would publish a daydream like those of Alnaschar and Malvolio. Those weaknesses which most men keep covered up in the most secret places of the mind, not to be disclosed to the eye of friendship or of love, were precisely the weaknesses which Boswell paraded before all the world. He was perfectly frank, because the weakness of his understanding and the tumult of his spirit prevented him from knowing when he made himself ridiculous. His book resembles nothing so much as the conversation of the inmates of the Palace of Truth.

His fame is great, and it will, we have no

Dr. Samuel Johnson

doubt, be lasting; but it is fame of a peculiar kind, and indeed marvelously resembles infamy. We remember no other case in which the world has made so great a distinction between a book and its author. In general, the book and the author are considered as one. To admire the book is to admire the author. The case of Boswell is an exception, we think the only exception, to this rule. His work is universally allowed to be interesting, instructive, eminently original; yet it has brought him nothing but contempt. All the world reads it, all the world delights in it; yet we do not remember ever to have read or even to have heard any expression of respect and admiration for the man to whom we owe so much instruction and amusement. While edition after edition of his book was coming forth, his son, as Mr. Croker tells us, was ashamed of it, and hated to hear it mentioned.

This feeling was natural and reasonable. Sir Alexander saw, that in proportion to the celebrity of the work was the degradation of the author. The very editors of this unfortunate gentleman's books have forgotten their allegiance, and, like those Puritan casuists who took arms by the authority of the king against his person, have attacked the writer while doing homage to the writings. Mr.

Dr. Samuel Johnson

Croker, for example, has published two thousand five hundred notes on the Life of Johnson, and yet scarcely ever mentions the biographer, whose performance he has taken such pains to illustrate, without some expression of contempt.

An ill-natured man Boswell certainly was not. Yet the malignity of the most malignant satirist could scarcely cut deeper than his thoughtless loquacity. Having himself no sensibility to derision and contempt, he took it for granted that all others were equally callous. He was not ashamed to exhibit himself to the whole world as a common spy, a common tattler, a humble companion without the excuse of poverty, to tell a hundred stories of his own pertness and folly, and of the insults which his pertness and folly brought upon him. It was natural that he should show little discretion in cases in which the feelings or the honor of others might be concerned. No man, surely, ever published such stories respecting persons whom he professed to love and revere. He would infallibly have made his hero as contemptible as he has made himself, had not this hero really possessed some moral and intellectual qualities of a very high order. The best proof that Johnson was really an extraordinary man,

Dr. Samuel Johnson

is, that his character, instead of being degraded, has, on the whole, been decidedly raised by a work in which all his vices and weaknesses are exposed more unsparingly than they ever were exposed by Churchill or by Kenrick.

His Character and Career

Johnson grown old, Johnson in the fulness of his fame and in the enjoyment of a competent fortune, is better known to us than any other man in history. Everything about him, his coat, his wig, his figure, his face, his scrofula, his St. Vitus's dance, his rolling walk, his blinking eye, the outward signs which too clearly marked his approbation of his dinner, his insatiable appetite for fish-sauce and veal-pie with plums, his inextinguishable thirst for tea, his trick of touching the posts as he walked, his mysterious practice of treasuring up scraps of orange-peel, his morning slumbers, his midnight disputations, his contortions, his mutterings, his gruntings, his puffings, his vigorous, acute, and ready eloquence, his sarcastic wit, his vehemence, his insolence, his fits of tempestuous rage, his queer inmates, old Mr. Levett and blind Mrs. Williams, the cat Hodge and the negro Frank—all are as

Dr. Samuel Johnson

familiar to us as the objects by which we have been surrounded from childhood. But we have no minute information respecting those years of Johnson's life during which his character and his manners became immutably fixed. We know him not as he was known to the men of his own generation, but as he was known to men whose father he might have been. That celebrated club of which he was the most distinguished member contained few persons who could remember a time when his fame was not fully established and his habits completely formed, He had made himself a name in literature while Reynolds and the Wartons were still boys. He was about twenty years older than Burke, Goldsmith, and Gerard Hamilton ; about thirty years older than Gibbon, Beauclerk, and Langton ; and about forty years older than Lord Stowell, Sir William Jones, and Windham. Boswell and Mrs. Thrale, the two writers from whom we derive most of our knowledge respecting him, never saw him till long after he was fifty years old, till most of his great works had become classical, and till the pension bestowed on him by Lord Bute had placed him above poverty. Of those eminent men who were his most intimate associates towards the close of his life, the only

Dr. Samuel Johnson

one, as far as we remember, who knew him during the first ten or twelve years of his residence in the capital, was David Garrick ; and it does not appear that, during those years, David Garrick saw much of his fellow townsman.

Johnson came up to London precisely at the time when the condition of a man of letters was most miserable and degraded. It was a dark night between two sunny days. The age of Mæcenases had passed away. The age of general curiosity and intelligence had not arrived. The number of readers is at present so great, that a popular author may subsist in comfort and opulence on the profits of his works. In the reigns of William the Third, of Anne, and of George the First, even such men as Congreve and Addison would scarcely have been able to live like gentlemen by the mere sale of their writings. But the deficiency of the natural demand for literature was, at the close of the seventeenth and at the beginning of the eighteenth century, more than made up by artificial encouragement, by a vast system of bounties and premiums. There was, perhaps, never a time at which the rewards of literary merit were so splendid —at which men who could write well found such easy admittance into the most distin-

Dr. Samuel Johnson

guished society and to the highest honors of the state. The chiefs of both the great parties into which the kingdom was divided patronized literature with emulous munificence. Congreve, when he had scarcely attained his majority, was rewarded for his first comedy with places which made him independent for life. Smith, though his Hippolytus and Phœdra failed, would have been consoled with £300 a year, but for his own folly. Rowe was not only poet-laureate, but land-surveyor of the customs in the port of London, clerk of the council to the Prince of Wales, and secretary of the Presentations to the Lord Chancellor. Hughes was secretary to the Commissions of the Peace. Ambrose Phillips was judge of the Prerogative Court in Ireland. Locke was Commissioner of Appeals and of the Board of Trade. Newton was master of the Mint. Stepney and Prior were employed in embassies of high dignity and importance. Gay, who commenced life as apprentice to a silk-mercer, became a secretary of legation at five-and-twenty. It was to a poem on the death of Charles II., and to the City and Country Mouse, that Montague owed his introduction into public life, his earldom, his garter, and his auditorship of the Exchequer. Swift, but for the unconquerable prejudice of the

Dr. Samuel Johnson

queen, would have been a bishop. Oxford, with his white staff in his hand, passed through the crowd of his suitors to welcome Parnell, when that ingenious writer deserted the Whigs, Steele was a commissioner of stamps and a member of Parliament. Arthur Mainwaring was a commissioner of the customs and auditor of the imprest. Tickell was secretary to the Lords Justices of Ireland. Addison was secretary of state.

This liberal patronage was brought into fashion, as it seems, by the magnificent Dorset, who alone, of all the noble versifiers in the court of Charles the Second, possessed talents for composition which would have made him, eminent without the aid of a coronet. Montague owed his elevation to the favor of Dorset, and imitated through the whole course of his life, the liberality to which he was himself so greatly indebted. The Tory leaders, Harley and Bolingbroke in particular, vied with the chiefs of the Whig party in zeal for the encouragement of letters. But soon after the accession of the house of Hanover a change took place. The supreme power passed to a man who cared little for poetry or eloquence. The importance of the House of Commons was constantly on the increase. The government was under the necessity of bartering,

Dr. Samuel Johnson

for parliamentary support, much of that patronage which had been employed in fostering literary merit; and Walpole was by no means inclined to divert any part of the fund of corruption to purposes which he considered as idle. He had eminent talents for government and for debate; but he had paid little attention to books, and felt little respect for authors. One of the coarse jokes of his friend, Sir Charles Hanbury Williams, was far more pleasing to him than Thomson's Seasons or Richardson's Pamela. He had observed that some of the distinguished writers whom the favor of Halifax had turned into statesmen, had been mere encumbrances to their party, dawdlers in office, and mutes in Parliament. During the whole course of his administration, therefore, he scarcely patronized a single man of genius. The best writers of the age gave all their support to the opposition, and contributed to excite that discontent which, after plunging the nation into a foolish and unjust war, overthrew the minister to make room for men less able and equally unscrupulous. The opposition could reward its eulogists with little more than promises and caresses. St. James would give nothing, Leicester-house had nothing to give.

Thus at the time when Johnson commenced

Dr. Samuel Johnson

his literary career, a writer had little to hope from the patronage of powerful individuals. The patronage of the public did not yet furnish the means of comfortable subsistence. The prices paid by booksellers to authors were so low, that a man of considerable talents and unremitting industry could do little more than provide for the day which was passing over him. The lean kine had eaten up the fat kine. The thin and withered ears had devoured the good ears. The season of rich harvest was over, and the period of famine had begun. All that is squalid and miserable might now be summed up in the one word—Poet. That word denoted a creature dressed like a scarecrow, familiar with compters and spunging-houses, and perfectly qualified to decide on the comparative merits of the Common Side in the King's Bench prison, and of Mount Scoundrel in the Fleet. Even the poorest pitied him; and they well might pity him. For if their condition was equally abject, their aspirings were not equally high, nor their sense of insult equally acute. To lodge in a garret up four pair of stairs, to dine in a cellar amongst footmen out of place; to translate ten hours a day for the wages of a ditcher; to be hunted by bailiffs from one haunt of beggary and pestilence to another,

Dr. Samuel Johnson

from Grub street to St. George's Fields, and from St. George's Fields to the alleys behind St. Martin's church; to sleep on a bulk in June, and amidst the ashes of a glasshouse in December, to die in an hospital, and to be buried in a parish vault, was the fate of more than one writer, who, if he had lived thirty years earlier, would have been admitted to the sittings of the Kit-Cat or the Scriblerus Club, would have sat in the Parliament, and would have been intrusted with embassies to the High Allies; who, if he had lived in our time, would have received from the booksellers several hundred pounds a year.

As every climate has its peculiar diseases, so every walk of life has its peculiar temptations. The literary character, assuredly, has always had its share of faults—vanity, jealousy, morbid sensibility. To these faults were now superadded all the faults which are commonly found in men whose livelihood is precarious, and whose principles are exposed to the trial of severe distress. All the vices of the gambler and of the beggar were blended with those of the author. The prizes in the wretched lottery of book-making were scarcely less ruinous than the blanks. If good fortune came it came in such a manner that it was almost certain to be abused. After months

Dr. Samuel Johnson

of starvation and despair, a full third night, or a well-received dedication, filled the pocket of the lean, ragged, unwashed poet with guineas. He hastened to enjoy those luxuries with the images of which his mind had been haunted while sleeping amidst the cinders, and eating potatoes at the Irish ordinary in Shoe Lane. A week of taverns soon qualified him for another year of night cellars. Such was the life of Savage, of Boyce, and of a crowd of others. Sometimes blazing in gold-laced hats and waistcoats, sometimes lying in bed because their coats had gone to pieces, or wearing paper cravats because their linen was in pawn ; sometimes drinking Champagne and Tokay with Betty Careless ; sometimes standing at the window of an eating-house in Porridge island, to snuff up the scent of what they could not afford to taste ; they knew luxury ; they knew beggary ; but they never knew comfort, These men were irreclaimable. They looked on a regular and frugal life with the same aversion which an old gipsy or a Mohawk hunter feels for a stationary abode, and for the restraints and securities of civilized communities. They were as untameable, as much wedded to their desolate freedom, 'as the wild ass. They could no more be broken in to the offices of social man

Dr. Samuel Johnson

than the unicorn could be trained to serve and abide by the crib. It was well, if they did not, like beasts of a still fiercer race, tear the hands which ministered to their necessities. To assist them was impossible; and the most benevolent of mankind at length became weary of giving relief, which was dissipated with the wildest profusion as soon as it had been received. If a sum was bestowed on the wretched adventurer, such as, properly husbanded, might have supplied him for six months, it was instantly spent in strange freaks of sensuality, and before forty-eight hours had elapsed, the poet was again pestering all his acquaintances for twopence to get a plate of shin of beef at a subterraneous cook-shop. If his friends gave him an asylum in their houses, those houses were forthwith turned into bagnios and taverns. All order was destroyed, all business was suspended. The most good-natured host began to repent of his eagerness to serve a man of genius in distress, when he heard his guest roaring for fresh punch at five o'clock in the morning.

A few eminent writers were more fortunate. Pope had been raised above poverty by the active patronage which, in his youth, both the great political parties had extended to his Homer. Young had received the only pension

Dr. Samuel Johnson

ever bestowed, to the best of our recollection, by Sir Robert Walpole, as the reward of mere literary merit. One or two of the many poets who attached themselves to the opposition, Thomson in particular, and Mallet, obtained, after much severe suffering, the means of subsistence from their political friends. Richardson, like a man of sense, kept his shop, and his shop kept him, which his novels, admirable as they are, would scarcely have done. But nothing could be more deplorable than the state even of the ablest men, who at that time depended for subsistence on their writings. Johnson, Collins, Fielding, and Thomson were certainly four of the most distinguished persons that England produced during the eighteenth century. It is well known that they were all four arrested for debt.

Into calamities and difficulties such as these Johnson plunged in his twenty-eighth year. From that time, till he was three or four-and-fifty, we have little information respecting him;—little, we mean, compared with the full and accurate information which we possess respecting his proceedings and habits towards the close of his life. He emerged at length from cocklofts and sixpenny ordinaries into the society of the polished and the opulent. His fame was established. A pension

Dr. Samuel Johnson

sufficient for his wants had been conferred on him; and he came forth to astonish a generation with which he had almost as little in common as with Frenchmen or Spaniards.

In his early years he had occasionally seen the great; but he had seen them as a beggar. He now came among them as a companion. The demand for amusement and instruction had, during the course of twenty years, been gradually increasing. The price of literary labors had risen; and those rising men of letters, with whom Johnson was henceforth to associate, were for the most part persons widely different from those who had walked about with him all night in the streets, for want of a lodging. Burke, Robertson, the Wartons, Gray, Mason, Gibbon, Adam Smith, Beattie, Sir William Jones, Goldsmith, and Churchill were the most distinguished writers of what may be called the second generation of the Johnsonian age. Of these men, Churchill was the only one in whom we can trace the stronger lineaments of that character, which, when Johnson first came up to London, was common among authors. Of the rest, scarcely any had felt the pressure of severe poverty. All had been early admitted into the most respectable society on an equal footing. They were men of quite a different

Dr. Samuel Johnson

species from the dependants of Curll and Osborne.

Johnson came among them the solitary specimen of a past age—the last survivor of a genuine race of Grub-street hacks; the last of that generation of authors whose abject misery and whose dissolute manners had furnished inexhaustible matter to the satirical genius of Pope. From nature, he had received an uncouth figure, a diseased constitution, and an irritable temper. The manner in which the earlier years of his manhood had been passed, had given to his demeanor, and even to his moral character, some peculiarities, appalling to the civilized beings who were the companions of his old age. The perverse irregularity of his hours, the slovenliness of his person, his fits of strenuous exertion, interrupted by long intervals of sluggishness; his strange abstinence, and his equally strange voracity; his active benevolence, contrasted with the constant rudeness and the occasional ferocity of his manners in society, made him, in the opinion of those with whom he lived during the last twenty years of his life, a complete original. An original he was, undoubtedly, in some respects. But if we possessed full information concerning those who shared his early hard-

Dr. Samuel Johnson

ships, we should probably find, that what we call his singularities of manner, were, for the most part, failings which he had in common with the class to which he belonged. He ate at Streatham Park as he had been used to eat behind the screen at St. John's Gate, when he was ashamed to show his ragged clothes. He ate as it was natural that a man should eat who, during a great part of his life, had passed the morning in doubt whether he should have food for the afternoon. The habits of his early life had accustomed him to bear privation with fortitude, but not to taste pleasure with moderation. He could fast; but when he did not fast he tore his dinner like a famished wolf, with the veins swelling on his forehead, and the perspiration running down his cheeks. He scarcely ever took wine. But when he drank it, he drank it greedily, and in large tumblers. These were, in fact, mitigated symptoms of that same moral disease, which raged with such deadly malignity in his friends Savage and Boyce. The roughness and violence which he showed in society were to be expected from a man whose temper, not naturally gentle, had been long tried by the bitterest calamities—by the want of meat, of fire, and of clothes; by the importunity of creditors, by the insolence of book-

Dr. Samuel Johnson

sellers, by the derision of fools, by the insincerity of patrons, by that bread which is the bitterest of all food, by those stairs which are the most toilsome of all paths, by that deferred hope which makes the heart sick. Through all these things the ill-dressed, coarse, ungainly pedant had struggled manfully up to eminence and command. It was natural, that, in the exercise of his power, he should be "eo immitior, quia toleraverat"— that though his heart was undoubtedly generous and humane, his demeanor in society should be harsh and despotic. For severe distress he had sympathy, and not only sympathy, but munificent relief. But for the suffering which a harsh word inflicts upon a delicate mind, he had no pity; for it was a kind of suffering which he could scarcely conceive. He would carry home on his shoulders a sick and starving girl from the streets. He turned his house into a place of refuge for a crowd of wretched old creatures who could find no other asylum; nor could all their peevishness and ingratitude weary out his benevolence. But the pangs of wounded vanity seemed to him ridiculous; and he scarcely felt sufficient compassion even for the pangs of wounded affection. He had seen and felt so much of sharp misery, that

Dr. Samuel Johnson

he was not affected by paltry vexations ; and he seemed to think that everybody ought to be as much hardened to those vexations as himself. He was angry with Boswell for complaining of a headache ; with Mrs. Thrale for grumbling about the dust on the road, or the smell of the kitchen. These were, in his phrase, "foppish lamentations," which people ought to be ashamed to utter in a world so full of misery. Goldsmith crying because the Good-natured Man had failed, inspired him with no pity. Though his own health was not good, he detested and despised valetudinarians. Even great pecuniary losses, unless they reduced the loser absolutely to beggary, moved him very little. People whose hearts had been softened by prosperity might cry, he said, for such events ; but all that could be expected of a plain man was not to laugh.

A person who troubled himself so little about the smaller grievances of human life, was not likely to be very attentive to the feelings of others in the ordinary intercourse of society. He could not understand how a sarcasm or a reprimand could make any man really unhappy. "My dear doctor," said he to Goldsmith, "what harm does it do to a man to call him Holofernes ?" "Poh, ma'am," he exclaimed to Mrs. Carter, "who is the

Dr. Samuel Johnson

worse for being talked of uncharitably?" Politeness has been well defined as benevolence in small things. Johnson was impolite, not because he wanted benevolence, but because small things appeared smaller to him than to people who had never known what it was to live for four-pence half-penny a day.

The characteristic peculiarity of his intellect was the union of great powers with low prejudices. If we judged of him by the best parts of his mind, we should place him almost as high as he was placed by the idolatry of of Boswell; if by the worst parts of his mind, we should place him even below Boswell himself. Where he was not under the influence of some strange scruple, or some domineering passion, which prevented him from boldly and fairly investigating a subject, he was a wary and accurate reasoner, a little too much inclined to skepticism, and a little too fond of paradox. No man was less likely to be imposed upon by fallacies in argument, or by exaggerated statements of fact. But, if, while he was beating down sophisms, and exposing false testimony, some childish prejudices, such as would excite laughter in a well-managed nursery, came across him, he was smitten as if by enchantment. His mind dwindled away under the spell from gigantic

Dr. Samuel Johnson

elevation to dwarfish littleness. Those who had lately been admiring its amplitude and its force, were now as much astonished at its strange narrowness and feebleness, as the fisherman, in the Arabian tale, when he saw the genie, whose stature had overshadowed the whole seacoast, and whose might seemed equal to a contest with armies, contract himself to the dimensions of his small prison, and lie there the helpless slave of the charm of Solomon.

Johnson was in the habit of sifting with extreme severity the evidence for all stories which were merely odd. But when they were not only odd but miraculous, his severity relaxed. He began to be credulous precisely at the point where the more credulous people begin to be skeptical. It is curious to observe, both in his writings and in his conversation, the contrast between the disdainful manner in which he rejects unauthenticated anecdotes, even when they are consistent with the general laws of nature, and the respectful manner in which he mentions the wildest stories relating to the invisible world. A man who told him of a waterspout or a meteoric stone generally had the lie direct given him for his pains. A man who told him of a prediction or a dream wonderfully accomplished, was

Dr. Samuel Johnson

sure of a courteous hearing. "Johnson," observes Hogarth, "like King David, says in his haste that all men are liars." "His incredulity," says Mrs. Thrale, "amounted almost to disease." She tells us how he browbeat a gentleman, who gave him an account of a hurricane in the West Indies, and a poor Quaker, who related some strange circumstance about the red-hot balls fired at the siege of Gibraltar. "It is not so. It cannot be true. Don't tell that story again. You cannot think how poor a figure you make in telling it." He once said, half jestingly we suppose, that for six months he refused to credit the fact of the earthquake at Lisbon, and that he still believed the extent of the calamity to be greatly exaggerated. Yet he related with a grave face how old Mr. Cave of St. John's Gate saw a ghost, and how this ghost was something of a shadowy being. He went himself on a ghost-hunt to Cocklane, and was angry with John Wesley for not following up another scent of the same kind with proper spirit and perseverance. He rejects the Celtic genealogies and poems without the least hesitation; yet he declares himself willing to believe the stories of the second sight. If he had examined the claims of the Highland seers with half the severity

Dr. Samuel Johnson

with which he sifted the evidence for the genuineness of Fingal, he would, we suspect, have come away from Scotland with a mind fully made up. In his Lives of the Poets, we find that he is unwilling to give credit to the accounts of Lord Roscommon's early proficiency in his studies ; but he tells with great solemnity an absurd romance about some intelligence preternaturally impressed on the mind of that nobleman. He avows himself to be in great doubt about the truth of the story, and ends by warning his readers not wholly to slight such impressions.

Many of his sentiments on religious subjects are worthy of a liberal and enlarged mind. He could discern clearly enough the folly and meanness of all bigotry except his own. When he spoke of the scruples of the Puritans, he spoke like a person who had really obtained an insight into the divine philosophy of the New Testament, and who considered Christianity as a noble scheme of government, tending to promote the happiness and to elevate the moral nature of man. The horror which the sectaries felt for cards, Christmas ale, plum-porridge, mince-pies, and dancing bears, excited his contempt. To the arguments urged by some very worthy people against showy dress, he replied with admirable sense and

Dr. Samuel Johnson

spirit, "Let us not be found, when our Master calls us, stripping the lace off our waistcoats, but the spirit of contention from our souls and tongues. Alas! sir, a man who cannot get to heaven in a green coat, will not find his way thither the sooner in a gray one." Yet he was himself under the tyranny of scruples as unreasonable as those of Hudibras or Ralpho; and carried his zeal for ceremonies and for ecclesiastical dignities to lengths altogether inconsistent with reason, or with Christian charity. He has gravely noted down in his diary, that he once committed the sin of drinking coffee on Good Friday. In Scotland, he thought it his duty to pass several months without joining in public worship, solely because the ministers of the kirk had not been ordained by bishops. His mode of estimating the piety of his neighbors was somewhat singular. "Campbell," said he, "is a good man—a pious man. I am afraid he has not been in the inside of a church for many years; but he never passes a church without pulling off his hat; this shows he has good principles." Spain and Sicily must surely contain many pious robbers and well-principled assassins. Johnson could easily see that a Roundhead, who named all his children after Solomon's singers, and talked in the House of Commons

Dr. Samuel Johnson

about seeking the Lord, might be an unprincipled villain, whose religious mummeries only aggravated his guilt. But a man who took off his hat when he passed a church episcopally consecrated, must be a good man, a pious man, a man of good principles. Johnson could easily see that those persons who looked on a dance or a laced waistcoat, as sinful, deemed most ignobly of the attributes of God, and of the ends of revelation. But with what a storm of invective he would have overwhelmed any man who had blamed him for celebrating the close of Lent with sugarless tea and butterless buns!

Nobody spoke more contemptuously of the cant of patriotism. Nobody saw more clearly the error of those who represented liberty, not as a means, but as an end; and who proposed to themselves, as the object of their pursuit, the prosperity of the state as distinct from the prosperity of the individuals who compose the state. His calm and settled opinion seems to have been that forms of government have little or no influence on the happiness of society. This opinion, erroneous as it is, ought at least to have preserved him from all intemperance on political questions. It did not, however, preserve him from the lowest, fiercest, and most absurd extrava-

Dr. Samuel Johnson

gance of party spirit—from rants which, in everything but the diction, resembled those of Squire Western. He was, as a politician, half ice and half fire—on the side of his intellect a mere Pococurante—far too apathetic about public affairs—far too skeptical as to the good or evil tendency of any form of polity. His passions, on the contrary, were violent even to slaying against all who leaned to Whiggish principles. The well-known lines which he inserted in Goldsmith's Traveller express what seems to have been his deliberate judgment:—

> " How small, of all that human hearts endure,
> That part which kings or laws can cause or cure."

He had previously put expressions very similar into the mouth of Rasselas. It is amusing to contrast these passages with the torrents of raving abuse which he poured forth against the Long Parliament and the American Congress. In one of the conversations reported by Boswell, this strange inconsistency displays itself in the most ludicrous manner.

"Sir Adam Ferguson," says Boswell, "suggested that luxury corrupts a people and destroys the spirit of liberty."—JOHNSON. "Sir, that is all visionary. I would not give half a guinea to live under one form of government rather than another. It is of no moment to the happiness of an individual.

Dr. Samuel Johnson

Sir, the danger of the abuse of power is nothing to a private man. What Frenchman is prevented from passing his life as he pleases?"—SIR ADAM. "But, sir, in the British constitution it is surely of importance to keep up a spirit in the people, so as to preserve a balance against the crown."—JOHNSON. "Sir, I perceive you are a vile Whig. Why all this childish jealousy of the power of the crown? The crown has not power enough."

One of the old philosophers, Lord Bacon tells us, used to say that life and death were just the same to him. "Why, then," said an objector, "do you not kill yourself?" The philosopher answered, "Because it is just the same." If the difference between two forms of government be not worth half a guinea, it is not easy to see how Whiggism can be viler than Toryism, or how the crown can have too little power. If private men suffer nothing from political abuses, zeal for liberty is doubtless ridiculous. But zeal for monarchy must be equally so. No person would have been more quick-sighted than Johnson to such a contradiction as this in the logic of an antagonist.

The judgments which Johnson passed on books were in his own time regarded with superstitious veneration; and in our time are generally treated with indiscriminate contempt. They are the judgments of a strong but enslaved understanding. The mind of

Dr. Samuel Johnson

the critic was hedged round by an uninterrupted fence of prejudices and superstitions. Within his narrow limits he displayed a vigor and an activity which ought to have enabled him to clear the barrier that confined him.

How it chanced that a man who reasoned on his premises so ably should assume his premises so foolishly, is one of the great mysteries of human nature. The same inconsistency may be observed in the schoolmen of the middle ages. Those writers show so much acuteness and force of mind in arguing on their wretched *data*, that a modern reader is perpetually at a loss to comprehend how such minds came by such *data*. Not a flaw in the superstructure of the theory which they are rearing escapes their vigilance. Yet they are blind to the obvious unsoundness of the foundation. It is the same with some eminent lawyers. Their legal arguments are intellectual prodigies, abounding with the happiest analogies and the most refined distinctions. The principles of their arbitrary science being once admitted, the statute-book and the reports being once assumed as the foundations of jurisprudence, these men must be allowed to be perfect masters of logic. But if a question arises as to the postulates on which their whole system rests, if they are called upon to

Dr. Samuel Johnson

vindicate the fundamental maxims of that system which they have passed their lives in studying, these very men often talk the language of savages or of children. Those who have listened to a man of this class in his own court, and who have witnessed the skill with which he analyzes and digests a vast mass of evidence, or reconciles a crowd of precedents which at first sight seem contradictory, scarcely know him again when, a few hours later, they hear him speaking on the other side of Westminster Hall in his capacity of legislator. They can scarcely believe that the paltry quirks which are faintly heard through a storm of coughing, and which cannot impose on the plainest country gentleman, can proceed from the same sharp and vigorous intellect which had excited their admiration under the same roof and on the same day.

Johnson decided literary questions like a lawyer, not like a legislator. He never examined foundations where a point was already ruled. His whole code of criticism rested on pure assumption, for which he sometimes gave a precedent or an authority, but rarely troubled himself to give a reason drawn from the nature of things. He took it for granted that the kind of poetry which flourished in his

Dr. Samuel Johnson

own time, which he had been accustomed to hear praised from his childhood, and which he had himself written with success, was the best kind of poetry. In his biographical work he has repeatedly laid it down as an undeniable proposition that, during the latter part of the seventeenth century and the earlier part of the eighteenth, English poetry had been in a constant progress of improvement. Waller, Denham, Dryden, and Pope had been, according to him, the great reformers. He judged of all works of the imagination by the standard established among his own contemporaries. Though he allowed Homer to have been a greater man than Virgil, he seems to have thought the Æneid a greater poem than the Iliad. Indeed he well might have thought so, for he preferred Pope's Iliad to Homer's. He pronounced that, after Hoole's translation of Tasso, Fairfax's would hardly be reprinted. He could see no merit in our fine old English ballads, and always spoke with the most provoking contempt of Percy's fondness for them. Of all the great original works which appeared during his time Richardson's novels alone excited his admiration. He could see little or no merit in Tom Jones, in Gulliver's Travels, or in Tristram Shandy. To Thomson's Castle of Indolence he vouchsafed only a line

Dr. Samuel Johnson

of cold commendation — of commendation much colder than what he has bestowed on the Creation of that portentous bore, Sir Richard Blackmore. Gray was, in his dialect, a barren rascal. Churchill was a blockhead. The contempt which he felt for the trash of Macpherson was indeed just; but it was, we suspect, just by chance. He despised the Fingal for the very reason which led many men of genius to admire it. He despised it, not because it was essentially commonplace, but because it had a superficial air of originality.

He was undoubtedly an excellent judge of compositions fashioned on his own principles. But when a deeper philosophy was required—when he undertook to pronounce judgment on the works of those great minds which "yield homage only to eternal laws"—his failure was ignominious. He criticised Pope's Epitaphs excellently. But his observations on Shakspeare's plays and Milton's poems seem to us as wretched as if they had been written by Rymer himself, whom we take to have been the worst critic that ever lived.

Some of Johnson's whims on literary subjects can be compared only to that strange, nervous feeling which made him uneasy if he had not touched every post between the

Dr. Samuel Johnson

Mitre tavern and his own lodgings. His preferences of Latin epitaphs to English epitaphs is an instance. An English epitaph, he said, would disgrace Smollett. He declared that he would not pollute the walls of Westminster Abbey with an English epitaph on Goldsmith. What reason there can be for celebrating a British writer in Latin which there was not for covering the Roman arches of triumph with Greek inscriptions, or for commemorating the deed of the heroes of Thermopylæ in Egyptian hieroglyphics, we are utterly unable to imagine.

On men and manners—at least, on the men and manners of a particular place and a particular age—Johnson had certainly looked with a most observant and discriminating eye. His remarks on the education of children, on marriage, on the economy of families, on the rules of society, are always striking, and generally sound. In his writings, indeed, the knowledge of life which he possessed in an eminent degree is very imperfectly exhibited. Like those unfortunate chiefs of the middle ages, who were suffocated by their own chain-mail and cloth of gold, his maxims perish under that load of words, which was designed for their ornament and their defence. But it is clear, from the remains of his conversa-

Dr. Samuel Johnson

tion, that he had more of that homely wisdom which nothing but experience and observation can give, than any writer since the time of Swift. If he had been content to write as he talked, he might have left books on the practical art of living superior to the Directions to Servants.

Yet even his remarks on society, like his remarks on literature, indicate a mind at least as remarkable for narrowness as for strength. He was no master of the great science of human nature. He had studied, not the *genus* man, but the *species* Londoner. Nobody was ever so thoroughly conversant with all the forms of life, and all the shades of moral and intellectual character, which were to be seen from Islington to the Thames, and from Hyde-Park corner to Mile-end green. But his philosophy stopped at the first turnpike gate. Of the rural life of England he knew nothing; and he took it for granted that everybody who lived in the country was either stupid or miserable. "Country gentlemen," said he, "must be unhappy; for they have not enough to keep their lives in motion." As if all those peculiar habits and associations, which made Fleet Street and Charing Cross the finest views in the world to himself, had been essential parts of human

Dr. Samuel Johnson

nature. Of remote countries and past times he talked with wild and ignorant presumption. "The Athenians of the age of Demosthenes," he said to Mrs. Thrale, "were a people of brutes, a barbarous people." In conversation with Sir Adam Ferguson he used similar language. "The boasted Athenians," he said, "were barbarians. The mass of every people must be barbarous, where there is no printing." The fact was this: he saw that a Londoner who could not read was a very stupid and brutal fellow: he saw that great refinement of taste and activity of intellect were rarely found in a Londoner who had not read much; and because it was by means of books that people acquired almost all their knowledge in the society with which he was acquainted, he concluded, in defiance of the strongest and clearest evidence, that the human mind can be cultivated by means of books alone. An Athenian citizen might possess very few volumes; and even the largest library to which he had access might be much less valuable than Johnson's bookcase in Bolt Court. But the Athenian might pass every morning in conversation with Socrates, and might hear Pericles speak four or five times every month. He saw the plays of Sophocles and Aristophanes; he walked

Dr. Samuel Johnson

amidst the friezes of Phidias and the paintings of Zeuxis ; he knew by heart the choruses of Æschylus ; he heard the rhapsodist at the corner of the street reciting the Shield of Achilles, or the Death of Argus ; he was a legislator conversant with high questions of alliance, revenue, and war ; he was a soldier, trained under a liberal and generous discipline ; he was a judge, compelled every day to weigh the effect of opposite arguments. These things were in themselves an education ; an education eminently fitted, not indeed to form exact or profound thinkers, but to give quickness to the perceptions, delicacy to the taste, fluency to the expression, and politeness to the manners. But this Johnson never considered, An Athenian who did not improve his mind by reading, was, in his opinion, much such a person as a Cockney who made his mark; much such a person as black Frank before he went to school, and far inferior to a parish-clerk or a printer's devil.

His friends have allowed that he carried to a ridiculous extreme his unjust contempt for foreigners. He pronounced the French to be a very silly people—much behind us—stupid, ignorant creatures. And this judgment he formed after having been at Paris about a month, during which he would not talk French, for fear of giving the natives an advantage over him in conversation. He pronounced them, also, to be an indelicate people, because a French footman touched the sugar with his fingers. That ingenious and amusing traveler, M. Simond, has defended his countrymen very successfully against Johnson's accusation, and has pointed out some English practices, which, to an impartial spectator, would seem at least as inconsistent with physical cleanliness and social decorum as those which Johnson so bitterly reprehended. To the sage, as Boswell loves to call him, it never occurred to doubt that there must be something eternally and immutably good in the usages to which he had been accustomed. In fact, Johnson's remarks on society beyond the bills of mortality, are generally of much the same kind with those of honest Tom Dawson, the English footman of Dr. Moore's Zeluco. "Suppose the King of France has no sons, but only a daughter, then, when the king dies, this here daughter, according to that there law, cannot be made queen, but the next near relative, provided he is a man, is made king, and not the last king's daughter, which, to be sure, is very unjust. The French footguards are dressed in blue, and

Dr. Samuel Johnson

all the marching regiments in white, which has a very foolish appearance for soldiers ; and as for blue regimentals, it is only fit for the blue horse or the artillery."

Johnson's visit to the Hebrides introduced him to a state of society completely new to him : and a salutary suspicion of his own deficiencies seems on that occasion to have crossed his mind for the first time. He confessed, in the last paragraph of his Journey, that his thoughts on national manners were the thoughts of one who had seen but little ; of one who had passed his time almost wholly in cities. This feeling, however, soon passed away. It is remarkable, that to the last he entertained a fixed contempt for all those modes of life and those studies, which lead to emancipate the mind from the prejudices of a particular age or a particular nation. Of foreign travel and of history he spoke with the fierce and boisterous contempt of ignorance. "What does a man learn by traveling ? Is Beauclerk the better for traveling ? What did Lord Charlemont learn in his travels, except that there was a snake in one of the pyramids of Egypt ?" History was, in his opinion, to use the fine expression of Lord Plunkett, an old almanac : historians could, as he conceived, claim no higher dignity than that of almanac-

Dr. Samuel Johnson

makers; and his favorite historians were those who, like Lord Hailes, aspired to no higher dignity. He always spoke with contempt of Robertson. Hume he would not even read. He affronted one of his friends for talking to him about Catiline's conspiracy, and declared that he never desired to hear of the Punic War again as long as he lived.

Assuredly one fact, which does not directly affect our own interests, considered in itself, is no better worth knowing than another fact. The fact that there is a snake in a pyramid, or the fact that Hannibal crossed the Alps by the Great St. Bernard, are in themselves as unprofitable to us as the fact that there is a green blind in a particular house in Threadneedle street, or the fact that a Mr. Smith comes into the city every morning on the top of one of the Blackwall stages. But it is certain that those who will not crack the shell of history will never get at the kernel. Johnson, with hasty arrogance, pronounced the kernel worthless, because he saw no value in the shell. The real use of traveling to distant countries, and of studying the annals of past times, is to preserve men from the contraction of mind which those can hardly escape, whose whole communion is with one generation and one neighborhood, who arrive at conclusions by

Dr. Samuel Johnson

means of an induction not sufficiently copious, and who therefore constantly confound exceptions with rules, and accidents with essential properties. In short, the real use of traveling, and of studying history, is to keep men from being what Tom Dawson was in fiction, and Samuel Johnson in reality.

Johnson, as Mr. Burke most justly observed, appears far greater in Boswell's books than in his own. His conversation appears to have been quite equal to his writings in matter, and far superior to them in manner. When he talked, he clothed his wit and his sense in forcible and natural expressions. As soon as he took his pen in his hand to write for the public, his style became systematically vicious. All his books are written in a learned language—in a language which nobody hears from his mother or his nurse—in a language in which nobody ever quarrels, or drives bargains, or makes love—in a language in which nobody ever thinks. It is clear, that Johnson himself did not think in the dialect in which he wrote. The expressions which came first to his tongue were simple, energetic, and picturesque. When he wrote for publication, he did his sentences out of English into Johnsonese. His letters from the Hebrides to Mrs. Thrale are the original of that work of which the

Dr. Samuel Johnson

Journey to the Hebrides as the translation; and it is amusing to compare the two versions. "When we were taken upstairs," says he in one of his letters, "a dirty fellow bounced out of the bed on which one of us was to lie," This incident is recorded in the Journey as follows: "Out of one of the beds on which we were to repose, started up, at our entrance, a man black as a Cyclops from the forge," Sometimes Johnson translated aloud. "The Rehearsal," he said, very unjustly, "has not wit enough to keep it sweet;" then, after a pause, "it has not vitality enough to preserve it from putrefaction."

Mannerism is pardonable, and is sometimes even agreeable, when the manner, though vicious, is natural. Few readers, for example, would be willing to part with the mannerism of Milton or of Burke. But a mannerism which does not sit easy on the mannerist, which has been adopted on principle, and which can be sustained only by constant effort, is always offensive. And such is the mannerism of Johnson.

The characteristic faults of his style are so familiar to all our readers, and have been so often burlesqued, that it is almost superfluous to point them out. It is well known that he made less use than any other eminent writer

Dr. Samuel Johnson

of those strong plain words, Anglo-Saxon or Norman French, of which the roots lie in the inmost depths of our language; and that he felt a vicious partiality for terms which, long after our own speech had been fixed, were borrowed from the Greek and Latin, and which, therefore, even when lawfully naturalized, must be considered as born aliens, not entitled to rank with the king's English. His constant practice of padding out a sentence with useless epithets, till it became as stiff as the bust of an exquisite; his antithetical forms of expression, constantly employed even where there is no opposition in the ideas expressed; his big words wasted on little things; his harsh inversions, so widely different from those graceful and easy inversions which give variety, spirit, and sweetness to the expression of our great old writers—all these peculiarities have been imitated by his admirers and parodied by his assailants, till the public has become sick of the subject.

Goldsmith said to him, very wittily and very justly, "If you were to write a fable about little fishes, doctor, you would make the little fishes talk like whales." No man surely ever had so little talent for personation as Johnson. Whether he wrote in the character of a disappointed legacy-hunter or an empty town

Dr. Samuel Johnson

fop, of a crazy virtuoso or a flippant coquette, he wrote in the same pompous and unbending style. His speech, like Sir Piercy Shafton's Euphuistic eloquence, bewrayed him under every disguise. Euphelia and Rhodoclia talk as finely as Imlac the poet, or Seged, Emperor of Ethiopia. The gay Cornelia describes her reception at the country-house of her relations in such terms as these: "I was surprised, after the civilities of my first reception, to find, instead of the leisure and tranquillity which a rural life always promises, and, if well conducted, might always afford, a confused wildness of care, and a tumultuous hurry of diligence, by which every face was clouded, and every motion agitated." The gentle Tranquilla informs us, that she "had not passed the early part of life without the flattery of courtship and the joys of triumph; but had danced the round of gayety amidst the murmurs of envy and the gratulations of applause; had been attended from pleasure to pleasure by the great, the sprightly, and the vain; and had seen her regard solicited by the obsequiousness of gallantry, the gayety of wit, and the timidity of love." Surely Sir John Falstaff himself did not wear his petticoats with a worse grace. The reader may well cry out with honest Sir Hugh

Dr. Samuel Johnson

Evans, "I like not when a 'oman has a great peard: I spy a great peard under her muffler."

We had something more to say. But our article is already too long; and we must close it. We would fain part in good humor from the hero, from the biographer, and even from the editor, who, ill as he has performed his task, has at least this claim to our gratitude, that he has induced us to read Boswell's book again. As we close it, the club-room is before us, and the table on which stands the omelet for Nugent and the lemons for Johnson. There are assembled those heads which live forever on the canvas of Reynolds. There are the spectacles of Burke and the tall thin form of Langton; the courtly sneer of Beauclerk and the beaming smile of Garrick; Gibbon tapping his snuff-box, and Sir Joshua with his trumpet in his ear. In the foreground is that strange figure which is as familiar to us as the figures of those among whom we have been brought up—the gigantic body, the huge massy face, seamed with the scars of disease; the brown coat, the black worsted stockings, the gray wig with a scorched foretop; the dirty hands, the nails bitten and pared to the quick. We see the eyes and mouth moving with convulsive twitches; we see the heavy form rolling; we

Dr. Samuel Johnson

hear it puffing ; and then comes the "Why, sir!" and the "What then, sir?" and the "No, sir!" and the "You don't see your way through the question, sir!"

What a singular destiny has been that of this remarkable man ! To be regarded in his own age as a classic, and in ours as a companion—to receive from his contemporaries that full homage which men of genius have in general received only from posterity—to be more intimately known to posterity than other men are known to their contemporaries ! That kind of fame which is commonly the most transient, is, in his case, the most durable. The reputation of those writings, which he probably expected to be immortal, is every day fading ; while those peculiarities of manner, and that careless table-talk, the memory of which, he probably thought, would die with him, are likely to be remembered as long as the English language is spoken in any quarter of the globe.

Lord Byron

From the essay on Moore's Life of Lord Byron, *Edinburgh Review*, June, 1831.

The Man

THE pretty fable by which the Duchess of Orleans illustrates the character of her son the regent might, with little change, be applied to Byron. All the fairies, save one, had been bidden to his cradle. All the gossips had been profuse of their gifts. One had bestowed nobility, another genius, a third beauty. The malignant elf who had been uninvited came last, and, unable to reverse what her sisters had done for their favorite, had mixed up a curse with every blessing. In the rank of Lord Byron, in his understanding, in his character, in his very person, there was a strange union of opposite extremes. He was born to all that men covet and admire. But in every one of those eminent advantages which he possessed over others, there was mingled something of misery and debasement. He was sprung from a house, ancient indeed and

Lord Byron

noble, but degraded and impoverished by a series of crimes and follies, which had attained a scandalous publicity. The kinsman whom he succeeded had died poor, and, but for merciful judges, would have died upon the gallows. The young peer had great intellectual powers; yet there was an unsound part in his mind. He had naturally a generous and tender heart; but his temper was wayward and irritable. He had a head which statuaries loved to copy, and a foot the deformity of which the beggars in the streets mimicked. Distinguished at once by the strength and by the weakness of his intellect, affectionate yet perverse, a poor lord, and a handsome cripple, he required, if ever man required, the firmest and the most judicious training. But, capriciously as nature had dealt with him, the relative to whom the office of forming his character was intrusted was more capricious still. She passed from paroxysms of rage to paroxysms of fondness. At one time she stifled him with her caresses, at another time she insulted his deformity. He came into the world, and the world treated him as his mother treated him—sometimes with kindness, sometimes with severity, never with justice. It indulged him without discrimination, and punished him without discrimi-

Lord Byron

nation. He was truly a spoiled child; not merely the spoiled child of his parents, but the spoiled child of nature, the spoiled child of fortune, the spoiled child of fame, the spoiled child of society. His first poems were received with a contempt which, feeble as they were, they did not absolutely deserve. The poem which he published on his return from his travels was, on the other hand, extolled far above its merits. At twenty-four, he found himself on the highest pinnacle of literary fame, with Scott, Wordsworth, Southey, and a crowd of other distinguished writers, beneath his feet. There is scarcely an instance in history of so sudden a rise to so dizzy an eminence.

Everything that could stimulate and everything that could gratify the strongest propensities of our nature—the gaze of a hundred drawing-rooms, the acclamations of the whole nation, the applause of applauded men, the love of the loveliest of women—all this world, and all the glory of it, were at once offered to a young man, to whom nature had given violent passions, and whom education had never taught to control them. He lived as many men live who have no similar excuses to plead for their faults. But his countrymen and his countrywomen would love him and admire him.

Lord Byron

They were resolved to see in his excesses only the flash and outbreak of that same fiery mind which glowed in his poetry. He attacked religion; yet in religious circles his name was mentioned with fondness, and in many religious publications his works were censured with singular tenderness. He lampooned the Prince Regent; yet he could not alienate the Tories. Everything, it seemed, was to be forgiven to youth, rank, and genius.

Then came the reaction. Society, capricious in its indignation, as it had been capricious in its fondness, flew into a rage with its froward and petted darling. He had been worshiped with an irrational idolatry. He was persecuted with an irrational fury. Much has been written about those unhappy domestic occurrences which decided the fate of his life. Yet nothing ever was positively known to the public, but this—that he quarreled with his lady, and that she refused to live with him. There have been hints in abundance, and shrugs and shakings of the head, and "Well, well, we know," and "We could an if we would," and "If we list to speak," and "There be that might an they list." But we are not aware that there is before the world, substantiated by credible, or even by tangible evidence, a single fact indicating that Lord

Lord Byron

Byron was more to blame than any other man who is on bad terms with his wife. The professional men whom Lady Byron consulted were undoubtedly of opinion that she ought not to live with her husband. But it is to be remembered that they formed that opinion without hearing both sides. We do not say, we do not mean to insinuate that Lady Byron was in any respect to blame. We think that those who condemn her on the evidence which is now before the public are as rash as those who condemn her husband. We will not pronounce any judgment ; we cannot, even in our own minds, form any judgment on a transaction which is so imperfectly known to us. It would have been well if, at the time of the separation, all those who knew as little about the matter then as we know about it now, had shown that forbearance, which, under such circumstances, is but common justice.

We know no spectacle so ridiculous as the British public in one of its periodical fits of morality. In general, elopements, divorces, and family quarrels pass with little notice. We read the scandal, talk about it for a day, and forget it. But once in six or seven years, our virtue becomes outrageous. We cannot suffer the laws of religion and decency to be violated. We must make a stand against vice. We must teach libertines that the English people appreciate the importance of domestic ties. Accordingly, some unfortunate man, in no respect more depraved than hundreds whose offenses have been treated with lenity, is singled out as an expiatory sacrifice. If he has children, they are to be taken from him. If he has a profession, he is to be driven from it. He is cut by the higher orders, and hissed by the lower. He is in truth, a sort of whipping-boy, by whose vicarious agonies all the other transgressors of the same class are, it is supposed, sufficiently chastised. We reflect very complacently on our own severity, and compare with great pride the high standard of morals established in England with the Parisian laxity. At length our anger is satiated. Our victim is ruined and heartbroken, and our virtue goes quietly to sleep for seven years more.

It is clear that those vices which destroy domestic happiness ought to be as much as possible repressed. It is equally clear that they cannot be repressed by penal legislation. It is therefore right and desirable that public opinion should be directed against them. But it should be directed against them uniformly, steadily, and temperately, not by

Lord Byron

sudden fits and starts. There should be one weight and one measure. Decimation is always an objectionable mode of punishment. It is the resource of judges too indolent and hasty to investigate facts and to discriminate nicely between shades of guilt. It is an irrational practice, even when adopted by military tribunals. When adopted by the tribunal of public opinion, it is infinitely more irrational. It is good that a certain portion of disgrace should constantly attend on certain bad actions; but it is not good that the offenders merely have to stand the risk of a lottery of infamy; that ninety-nine out of every hundred should escape, and that the hundredth, perhaps the most innocent of the hundred, should pay for all. We remember to have seen a mob assembled in Lincoln's Inn to hoot a gentleman, against whom the most oppressive proceeding known to the English law was then in progress. He was hooted because he had been an indifferent and unfaithful husband, as if some of the most popular men of the age, Lord Nelson, for example, had not been indifferent and unfaithful husbands. We remember a still stronger case. Will posterity believe, that in an age in which men, whose gallantries were universally known, and had been legally proved, filled some of the highest

Lord Byron

offices in the state and in the army, presided at the meetings of religious and benevolent institutions, were the delight of every society and the favorites of the multitude, a crowd of moralists went to the theater, in order to pelt a poor actor for disturbing the conjugal felicty of an alderman? What there was in the circumstances, either of the offender, or of the sufferer, to vindicate the zeal of the audience, we could never conceive. It has never been supposed that the situation of an actor is peculiarly favorable to the rigid virtues, or that an alderman enjoys any special immunity from injuries such as that which on this occasion roused the anger of the public. But such is the justice of mankind.

In these cases, the punishment was excessive; but the offense was known and proved. The case of Lord Byron was harder, True Jedwood justice was dealt out to him. First came the execution, then the investigation, and last of all, or rather not at all, the accusation. The public, without knowing anything whatever about the transactions in his family, flew into a violent passion with him, and proceeded to invent stories which might justify its anger. Ten or twenty different accounts of the separation, inconsistent with each other, with themselves, and with common

Lord Byron

sense, circulated at the same time. What evidence there might be for any one of these, the virtuous people who repeated them neither knew nor cared. For in fact these stories were not the causes, but the effects of the public indignation. They resembled those loathsome slanders which Goldsmith, and other abject libelers of the same class were in the habit of publishing about Bonaparte—how he poisoned a girl with arsenic, when he was at the military school—how he hired a grenadier to shoot Dessaix at Marengo—how he filled St. Cloud with all the pollutions of Capreæ. There was a time when anecdotes like these obtained some credence from persons, who, hating the French Emperor, without knowing why, were eager to believe anything which might justify their hatred. Lord Byron fared in the same way. His countrymen were in a bad humor with him. His writings and his character had lost the charm of novelty. He had been guilty of the offense which, of all offenses, is punished more severely; he had been over-praised; he had excited too warm an interest: and the public, with its usual justice, chastised him for its own folly. The attachments of the multitude bear no small resemblance to those of the wanton enchantress in the Arabian

Lord Byron

Tales, who, when the forty days of her fondness were over, was not content with dismissing her lovers, but condemned them to expiate, in loathsome shapes, and under severe punishments, the crime of having once pleased her too well.

The obloquy which Byron had to endure was such as might well have shaken a more constant mind. The newspapers were filled with lampoons. The theaters shook with execrations. He was excluded from circles where he had lately been the observed of all observers. All those creeping things, that riot in the decay of nobler natures, hastened to their repast; and they were right; they did after their kind. It is not every day that the savage envy of aspiring dunces is gratified by the agonies of such a spirit, and the degradation of such a name.

The unhappy man left his country for ever. The howl of contumely followed him across the sea, up the Rhine, over the Alps; it gradually waxed fainter; it died away. Those who had raised it, began to ask each other, what, after all, was the matter about which they had been so clamorous; and wished to invite back the criminal whom they had just chased from them. His poetry became more popular than it ever had been; and his complaints were read with tears by thousands and tens of thousands who had never seen his face.

He had fixed his home on the shores of the Adriatic, in the most picturesque and interesting of cities, beneath the brightest of skies, and by the brightest of seas. Censoriousness was not the vice of the neighbors whom he had chosen. They were a race corrupted by a bad government and a bad religion ; long renowned for skill in the arts of voluptuousness, and tolerant of all the caprices of sensuality. From the public opinion of the country of his adoption he had nothing to dread. With the public opinion of the country of his birth he was at open war. He plunged into wild and desperate excesses, ennobled by no generous or tender sentiment. From his Venetian harem, he sent forth volume after volume, full of eloquence, of wit, of pathos, of ribaldry, and of bitter disdain. His health sank under the effects of his intemperance. His hair turned gray. His food ceased to nourish him. A hectic fever withered him up. It seemed that his body and mind were about to perish together.

From this wretched degradation he was in some measure rescued by an attachment, culpable indeed, yet such as, judged by the

Lord Byron

standard of morality established in the country where he lived, might be called virtuous. But an imagination polluted by vice, a temper imbittered by misfortune, and a frame habituated to the fatal excitement of intoxication, prevented him from fully enjoying the happiness which he might have derived from the purest and most tranquil of his many attachments. Midnight draughts of ardent spirits and Rhenish wines had begun to work the ruin of his fine intellect. His verse lost much of the energy and condensation which had distinguished it. But he would not resign, without a struggle, the empire which he had exercised over the men of his generation. A new dream of ambition arose before him, to be the center of a literary party ; the great mover of an intellectual revolution ; to guide the public mind of England from his Italian retreat, as Voltaire had guided the public mind of France from the villa of Ferney. With this hope, as it should seem, he established *The Liberal.* But, powerfully as he had affected the imaginations of his contemporaries, he mistook his own powers, if he hoped to direct their opinions : and he still more grossly mistook his own disposition, if he thought that he could long act in concert with other men of letters. The plan failed, and failed ignominiously. Angry

Lord Byron

with himself, angry with his coadjutors, he relinquished it; and turned to another project, the last and the noblest of his life.

A nation, once the first among the nations, pre-eminent in knowledge, pre-eminent in military glory, the cradle of philosophy, of eloquence, and of the fine arts, had been for ages bowed down under a cruel yoke. All the vices which tyranny generates—the abject vices which it generates in those who submit to it, the ferocious vices which it generates in those who struggle against it—had deformed the character of that miserable race. The valor which had won the great battle of human civilization, which had saved Europe, and subjugated Asia, lingered only among pirates and robbers. The ingenuity, once so conspicuously displayed in every department of physical and moral science, had been depraved into a timid and servile cunning. On a sudden, this degraded people had risen on their oppressors. Discountenanced or betrayed by the surrounding potentates, they had found in themselves something of that which might well supply the place of all foreign assistance—something of the energy of their fathers.

As a man of letters, Lord Byron could not but be interested in the event of his contest.

Lord Byron

His political opinions, though, like all his opinions, unsettled, leaned strongly towards the side of liberty. He had assisted the Italian insurgents with his purse; and if their struggle against the Austrian government had been prolonged, would probably have assisted them with his sword. But to Greece he was attached by peculiar ties. He had, when young, resided in that country. Much of his most splendid and popular poetry had been inspired by its scenery and by its history. Sick of inaction, degraded in his own eyes by his private vices and by his literary failures, pining for untried excitement and honorable distinction, he carried his exhausted body and his wounded spirit to the Grecian camp.

His conduct in his new situation showed so much vigor and good sense as to justify us in believing, that, if his life had been prolonged, he might have distinguished himself as a soldier and a politician. But pleasure and sorrow had done the work of seventy years upon his delicate frame. The hand of death was on him; he knew it; and the only wish which he uttered was that he might die sword in hand.

This was denied to him. Anxiety, exertion, exposure, and those fatal stimulants which had become indispensable to him,

Lord Byron

soon stretched him on a sick-bed, in a strange land, amidst strange faces, without one human being that he loved near him. There, at thirty-six, the most celebrated Englishman of the nineteenth century closed his brilliant and miserable career.

The Poet

Lord Byron, like Mr. Wordsworth, had nothing dramatic in his genius. He was, indeed, the reverse of a great dramatist—the very antithesis to a great dramatist. All his characters—Harold looking back on the western sky, from which his country and the sun are receding together; the Giaour, standing apart in the gloom of the side-aisle, and casting a haggard scowl from under his long hood at the crucifix and the censer; Conrad, leaning on his sword by the watch-tower; Lara, smiling on the dancers; Alp, gazing steadily on the fatal cloud as it passes before the moon; Manfred, wandering among the precipices of Berne; Azo, on the judgment-seat; Ugo, at the bar; Lambro, frowning on the siesta of his daughter and Juan; Cain, presenting his unacceptable offering—all are essentially the same. The varieties are varieties merely of age, situation, and costume. If ever Lord Byron attempted to exhibit men

Lord Byron

of a different kind, he always made them either insipid or unnatural. Selim is nothing. Bonnivart is nothing. Don Juan, in the first and best cantos, is a feeble copy of the Page in the Marriage of Figaro. Johnson, the man whom Juan meets in the slave-market, is a most striking failure, How differently would Sir Walter Scott have drawn a bluff, fearless Englishman in such a situation! The portrait would have seemed to walk out of the canvas.

Sardanapalus is more hardly drawn than any dramatic personage than we can remember. His heroism and his effeminacy, his contempt of death, and his dread of a weighty helmet, his kingly resolution to be seen in the foremost ranks, and the anxiety with which he calls for a looking-glass, that he may be seen to advantage, are contrasted with all the point of Juvenal. Indeed, the hint of the character seems to have been taken from what Juvenal says of Otho,—

> "Speculum civilis sarcina belli.
> Nimirum summi ducis est occidere Galbam.
> Et curare cutem; summi constantia civis
> Bebriaci campo spolium affectare Palati,
> Et pressum in faciem digitis extendere panem."

These are excellent lines in a satire. But it is not the business of the dramatist to exhibit

Lord Byron

characters in this sharp, antithetical way. It is not in this way that Shakspeare makes Prince Hal rise from the rake of Eastcheap into the hero of Shrewsbury, and sink again into the rake of Eastcheap. It is not thus that Shakspeare has exhibited the union of effeminacy and valor in Antony. A dramatist cannot commit a greater error than that of following those pointed descriptions of character in which satirists and historians indulge so much. It is by rejecting what is natural that satirists and historians produce these striking characters. Their great object generally is to ascribe to every man as many contradictory qualities as possible; and this is an object easily attained. By judicious selections and judicious exaggeration, the intellect and the disposition of any human being might be described as being made up of nothing but startling contrasts. If the dramatist attempts to create a being answering to one of these descriptions, he fails; because he reverses an imperfect analytical process. He produces, not a man, but a personified epigram. Very eminent writers have fallen into this snare. Ben Johnson has given us an Hermogenes taken from the lively lines of Horace; but the inconsistency which is so amusing in the satire appears unnatural and

Lord Byron

disgusts us in the play. Sir Walter Scott has committed a far more glaring error of the same kind, in the novel of Peveril. Admiring, as every reader must admire, the keen and vigorous lines in which Dryden satirized the Duke of Buckingham, he attempted to make a Duke of Buckingham to suit them—a real living Zimri; and he made, not a man, but the most grotesque of all monsters. A writer who should attempt to introduce into a play or a novel such a Wharton as the Wharton of Pope, or a Lord Hervey answering to Sporus, would fail in the same manner.

But to return to Lord Byron: his women, like his men, are all of one breed. Haidee is a half-savage and girlish Julia; Julia is a civilized and matronly Haidee. Leila is a wedded Zuleika—Zuleika a virgin Leila. Gulnare and Medora appear to have been intentionally opposed to each other; yet the difference is a difference of situation only. A slight change of circumstance would, it should seem, have sent Gulnare to the lute of Medora, and armed Medora with the dagger of Gulnare.

It is hardly too much to say that Lord Byron could exhibit only one man and only one woman—a man proud, moody, cynical, with defiance on his brow, and misery in his

Lord Byron

heart; a scorner of his kind, implacable in revenge, yet capable of deep and strong affection;—a woman all softness and gentleness, loving to caress and to be caressed, but capable of being transformed by love into a tigress.

Even these two characters, his only two characters, he could not exhibit dramatically. He exhibited them in the manner, not of Shakspeare, but of Clarendon. He analyzed them. He made them analyze themselves, but he did not make them show themselves. He tells us, for example, in many lines of great force and spirit, that the speech of Lara was bitterly sarcastic, that he talked little of his travels, that if much questioned about them, his answers became short, and his brow gloomy. But we have none of Lara's sarcastic speeches, or short answers. It is not thus that the great masters of human nature have portrayed human beings. Homer never tells us that Nestor loved to tell long stories about his youth; Shakspeare never tells us that in the mind of Iago everything that is beautiful and endearing was associated with some filthy and debasing idea.

It is curious to observe the tendency which the dialogue of Lord Byron always has to lose its character of dialogue, and to become soliloquy. The scenes between Manfred and

Lord Byron

the Chamois-hunter, between Manfred and the Witch of the Alps, between Manfred and the Abbot, are instances of this tendency. Manfred, after a few unimportant speeches, has all the talk to himself. The other interlocutors are nothing more than good listeners. They drop an occasional question, or ejaculation, which sets Manfred off again on the inexhaustible topic of his personal feelings. If we examine the fine passages in Lord Byron's dramas, the description of Rome, for example, in Manfred, the description of a Venetian revel in Marino Faliero, the dying invective which the old Doge pronounces against Venice, we shall find there is nothing dramatic in them; that they derive none of their effect from the character or situation of the speaker; and that they would have been as fine, or finer, if they had been published as fragments of blank verse by Lord Byron. There is scarcely a speech in Shakspeare of which the same could be said. No skilful reader of the plays of Shakspeare can endure to see what are called the fine things taken out, under the name of "Beauties," or of "Elegant Extracts;" or to hear any single passage—"To be or not to be," for example, quoted as a sample of the great poet. "To be or not to be" has merit undoubtedly as a

Lord Byron

composition. It would have merit if put into the mouth of a chorus. But its merit as a composition vanishes when compared with its merit as belonging to Hamlet. It is not too much to say that the great plays of Shakspeare would lose less by being deprived of all the passages which are commonly called the fine passages, than those passages lose by being read separately from the play. This is perhaps the highest praise which can be given to a dramatist.

On the other hand, it may be doubted whether there is, in all Lord Byron's plays, a single remarkable passage which owes any portion of its interest or effect to its connection with the characters or the action. He has written only one scene, as far as we can recollect, which is dramatic even in manner—the scene between Lucifer and Cain. The conference in that scene is animated, and each of the interlocutors has a fair share of it. But this scene, when examined, will be found to be a confirmation of our remarks. It is a dialogue only in form. It is a soliloquy in essence. It is in reality a debate carried on within one single, unquiet, and skeptical mind. The questions and the answers, the objections and the solutions, all belong to the same character.

Lord Byron

A writer who showed so little of dramatic skill in works professedly dramatic was not likely to write narrative with dramatic effect. Nothing could indeed be more rude and careless than the structure of his narrative poems. He seems to have thought, with the hero of the Rehearsal, that the plot was good for nothing but to bring in fine things. His two longest works, Childe Harold and Don Juan, have no plan whatever. Either of them might have been extended to any length, or cut short at any point. The state in which the Giaour appears illustrates the manner in which all his poems were constructed. They are all, like the Giaour, collections of fragments; and, though there may be no empty spaces marked by asterisks, it is still easy to perceive, by the clumsiness of the joining, where the parts, for the sake of which the whole was composed, end and begin.

It was in description and meditation that he excelled. "Description," as he said in Don Juan, "was his *forte*." His manner is indeed peculiar, and is almost unequaled—rapid, sketchy, full of vigor; the selection happy; the strokes few and bold. In spite of the reverence which we feel for the genius of Mr. Wordsworth, we cannot but think that the minuteness of his descriptions often dimin-

Lord Byron

ishes their effect. He has accustomed himself to gaze on nature with the eye of a lover —to dwell on every feature, and to mark every change of aspect. Those beauties which strike the most negligent observer, and those which only a close attention discovers, are equally familiar to him, and are equally prominent in his poetry. The proverb of old Hesiod, that half is often more than the whole, is eminently applicable to description. The policy of the Dutch, who cut down most of the precious trees in the Spice Islands, in order to raise the value of what remained, was a policy which poets would do well to imitate. It was a policy which no poet understood better than Lord Byron. Whatever his faults might be, he was never, while his mind retained its vigor, accused of prolixity,

His descriptions, great as was their intrinsic merit, derived their principal interest from the feeling which always mingled with them. He was himself the beginning, the middle, and the end of all his own poetry, the hero of every tale, the chief object in every landscape. Harold, Lara, Manfred, and a crowd of other characters, were universally considered merely as loose incognitos of Byron ; and there is every reason to believe that he meant them to be so considered.

Lord Byron

The wonders of the outer world, the Tagus, with the mighty fleets of England riding on its bosom, the towers of Cintra overhanging the shaggy forest of cork-trees and willows, the glaring marble of Pentelicus, the banks of the Rhine, the glaciers of Clarens, the sweet Lake of Leman, the dell of Egeria, with its summer-birds and rustling lizards, the shapeless ruins of Rome, overgrown with ivy and wall-flowers, the stars, the sea, the mountains —all were mere accessaries—the background to one dark and melancholy figure.

Never had any writer so vast a command of the whole eloquence of scorn, misanthropy, and despair. That Marah was never dry. No art could sweeten, no draughts could exhaust its perennial waters of bitterness. Never was there such variety in monotony as that of Byron. From maniac laughter to piercing lamentation, there was not a single note of human anguish of which he was not master. Year after year, and month after month, he continued to repeat that to be wretched is the destiny of all ; that to be eminently wretched is the destiny of the eminent ; that all the desires by which we are cursed lead alike to misery ;—if they are not gratified, to the misery of disappointment ; if they are gratified, to the misery of satiety. His

Lord Byron

principal heroes are men who have arrived by different roads at the same goal of despair, who are sick of life, who are at war with society, who are supported in their anguish only by an unconquerable pride, resembling that of Prometheus on the rock, or of Satan in the burning marl; who can master their agonies by the force of their will, and who, to the last, defy the whole power of earth and heaven. He always described himself as a man of the same kind with his favorite creations, as a man whose heart has been withered, whose capacity for happiness was gone, and could not be restored; but whose invincible spirit dared the worst that could befall him here or hereafter.

How much of this morbid feeling sprung from an original disease of mind, how much from real misfortune, how much from the nervousness of dissipation, how much of it was fanciful, how much of it was merely affected, it is impossible for us, and would probably have been impossible for the most intimate friends of Lord Byron to decide. Whether there ever existed, or can ever exist, a person answering to the description which he gave of himself, may be doubted: but that he was not such a person is beyond all doubt. It is ridiculous to imagine that a

Lord Byron

man whose mind was really imbued with scorn of his fellow-creatures would have published three or four books every year in order to tell them so ; or that a man, who could say with truth that he neither sought sympathy nor needed it, would have admitted all Europe to hear his farewell to his wife, and his blessings on his child. In the second canto of Childe Harold, he tells us that he is insensible to fame and obloquy :

> "Ill may such contest now the spirit move.
> Which heeds nor keen reproof nor partial praise."

Yet we know, on the best evidence, that a day or two before he published these lines, he was greatly, indeed childishly, elated by the compliments paid to his maiden speech in the House of Lords.

We are far, however, from thinking that his sadness was altogether feigned. He was naturally a man of great sensibility ; he had been ill-educated ; his feelings had been early exposed to sharp trials ; he had been crossed in his boyish love ; he had been mortified by the failure of his first literary efforts ; he was straitened in pecuniary circumstances ; he was unfortunate in his domestic relations ; the public treated him with cruel injustice ; his health and spirits

Lord Byron

suffered from his dissipated habits of life; he was, on the whole, an unhappy man. He early discovered that, by parading his unhappiness before the multitude, he excited an unrivaled interest. The world gave him every encouragement to talk about his mental sufferings. The effect which his first confessions produced induced him to affect much that he did not feel; and the affectation probably reacted on his feelings. How far the character in which he exhibited himself was genuine, and how far theatrical, would probably have puzzled himself to say.

There can be no doubt that this remarkable man owed the vast influence which he exercised over his contemporaries at least as much to his gloomy egotism as to the real power of his poetry. We never could very clearly understand how it is that egotism, so unpopular in conversation, should be so popular in writing; or how it is that men who affect in their compositions qualities and feelings which they have not, impose so much more easily on their contemporaries than on posterity. The interest which the loves of Petrarch excited in his own time, and the pitying fondness with which half Europe looked upon Rousseau, are well known. To readers of our time, the love of Petrarch

Lord Byron

seems to have been love of that kind which breaks no hearts ; and the sufferings of Rousseau to have deserved laughter rather than pity—to have been partly counterfeited, and partly the consequences of his own perverseness and vanity.

What our grandchildren may think of the character of Lord Byron as exhibited in his poetry, we will not pretend to guess. It is certain, that the interest which he excited during his life is without a parallel in literary history. The feeling with which young readers of poetry regarded him can be conceived only by those who have experienced it. To people who are unacquainted with the real calamity, "nothing is so dainty sweet as lovely melancholy." This faint image of sorrow has in all ages been considered by young gentlemen as an agreeable excitement. Old gentlemen and middle-aged gentlemen have so many real causes of sadness, that they are rarely inclined "to be as sad as night only for wantonness." Indeed they want the power almost as much as the inclination. We know very few persons engaged in active life, who even if they were to procure stools to be melancholy upon, and were to sit down with all the premeditation of Master Stephen, would be able to enjoy

Lord Byron

much of what somebody calls "the ecstasy of wo."

Among that large class of young persons whose reading is almost entirely confined to works of imagination, the popularity of Lord Byron was unbounded. They bought pictures of him, they treasured up the smallest relics of him; they learned his poems by heart, and did their best to write like him, and to look like him. Many of them practised at the glass, in the hope of catching the curl of the upper lip, and the scowl of the brow, which appear in some of his portraits. A few discarded their neckcloths, in imitation of their great leader. For some years, the Minerva press sent forth no novel without a mysterious, unhappy Lara-like peer. The number of hopeful undergraduates and medical students who became things of dark imaginings, on whom the freshness of the heart ceased to fall like dew, whose passions had consumed themselves to dust, and to whom the relief of tears was denied, passes all calculation. This was not the worst. There was created in the minds of many of these enthusiasts a pernicious and absurd association between intellectual power and moral depravity. From the poetry of Lord Byron they drew a system of ethics, com-

Lord Byron

pounded of misanthropy and voluptuousness; a system in which the two great commandments were, to hate your neighbor, and to love your neighbor's wife.

This affectation has passed away; and a few more years will destroy whatever yet remains of that magical potency which once belonged to the name of Byron. To us he is still a man, young, noble and unhappy. To our children he will be merely a writer; and their impartial judgment will appoint his place among writers, without regard to his rank, or to his private history. That his poetry will undergo a severe sifting; that much of what has been admired by his contemporaries will be rejected as worthless, we have little doubt. But we have as little doubt, that, after the closest scrutiny there will still remain much that can only perish with the English language.

England under the Restoration

From the "History of England," Chapter III

The Country Gentlemen

We should be much mistaken if we pictured to ourselves the squires of the seventeenth century as men bearing a close resemblance to their descendants, the county members and chairmen of quarter sessions with whom we are familiar. The modern country gentleman generally receives a liberal education, passes from a distinguished school to a distinguished college, and has ample opportunity to become an excellent scholar. He has generally seen something of foreign countries. A considerable part of his life has generally been passed in the capital; and the refinements of the capital follow him into the country. There is perhaps no class of dwellings so pleasing as the rural seats of the English gentry. In the parks and pleasure grounds, nature, dressed yet not disguised by art, wears her most alluring form. In the buildings, good

England under the Restoration

sense and good taste combine to produce a happy union of the comfortable and the graceful. The pictures, the musical instruments, the library, would in any other country be considered as proving the owner to be an eminently polished and accomplished man. A country gentleman who witnessed the Revolution was probably in receipt of about a fourth part of the rent which his acres now yield to his posterity. He was, therefore, as compared with his posterity, a poor man, and was generally under the necessity of residing, with little interruption, on his estate. To travel on the Continent, to maintain an establishment in London, or even to visit London frequently, were pleasures in which only the great proprietors could indulge. It may be confidently affirmed that of the squires whose names were then in the Commissions of Peace and Lieutenancy not one in twenty went to town once in five years, or had ever in his life wandered so far as Paris. Many lords of manors had received an education differing little from that of their menial servants. The heir of an estate often passed his boyhood and youth at the seat of his family with no better tutors than grooms and gamekeepers, and scarce attained learning enough to sign his name to a Mittimus. If he went to school and to col-

England under the Restoration

lege, he generally returned before he was twenty to the seclusion of the old hall, and there, unless his mind were very happily constituted by nature, soon forgot his academical pursuits in rural business and pleasures. His chief serious employment was the care of his property. He examined samples of grain, handled pigs, and, on market days made bargains over a tankard with drovers and hop merchants. His chief pleasures were commonly derived from field sports and from an unrefined sensuality. His language and pronunciation were such as we should now expect to hear only from the most ignorant clowns. His oaths, coarse jests, and scurrilous terms of abuse, were uttered with the broadest accent of his province. It was easy to discern, from the first words which he spoke, whether he came from Somersetshire or Yorkshire. He troubled himself little about decorating his abode, and, if he attempted decoration, seldom produced anything but deformity. The litter of a farmyard gathered under the windows of his bedchamber, and the cabbages and gooseberry bushes grew close to his hall door. His table was loaded with coarse plenty; and guests were cordially welcomed to it. But, as the habit of drinking to excess was general in the class to which he

England under the Restoration

belonged, and as his fortune did not enable him to intoxicate large assemblies daily with claret or canary, strong beer was the ordinary beverage. The quantity of beer consumed in those days was indeed enormous. For beer then was to the middle and lower classes, not only all that beer is, but all that wine, tea, and ardent spirits now are. It was only at great houses, or on great occasions, that foreign drink was placed on the board. The ladies of the house, whose business it had commonly been to cook the repast, retired as soon as the dishes had been devoured, and left the gentlemen to their ale and tobacco. The coarse jollity of the afternoon was often prolonged till the revelers were laid under the table.

It was very seldom that the country gentleman caught glimpses of the great world; and what he saw of it tended rather to confuse than to enlighten his understanding. His opinions respecting religion, government, foreign countries and former times, having been derived, not from study, from observation, or from conversation with enlightened companions, but from such traditions as were current in his own small circle, were the opinions of a child. He adhered to them, however, with the obstinacy which is generally

England under the Restoration

found in ignorant men accustomed to be fed with flattery. His animosities were numerous and bitter. He hated Frenchmen and Italians, Scotchmen and Irishmen, Papists and Presbyterians, Independents and Baptists, Quakers and Jews. Towards London and Londoners he felt an aversion which more than once produced important political effects. His wife and daughter were in tastes and acquirements below a housekeeper or a stillroom maid of the present day. They stitched and spun, brewed gooseberry wine, cured marigolds, and made the crust for the venison pasty.

From this description it might be supposed that the English esquire of the seventeenth century did not materially differ from a rustic miller or alehouse keeper of our time. There are, however, some important parts of his character still to be noted, which will greatly modify this estimate. Unlettered as he was and unpolished he was still in some most important points a gentleman. He was a member of a proud and powerful aristocracy, and was distinguished by many both of the good and of the bad qualities which belong to aristocrats. His family pride was beyond that of a Talbot or a Howard. He knew the genealogies and coats of arms of all his neighbors, and could tell

England under the Restoration

which of them had assumed supporters without any right, and which of them were so unfortunate as to be great-grandsons of aldermen. He was a magistrate, and, as such, administered gratuitously to those who dwelt around him a rude patriarchal justice, which, in spite of innumerable blunders and of occasional acts of tyranny, was yet better than no justice at all. He was an officer of the trainbands; and his military dignity, though it might move the mirth of gallants who had served a campaign in Flanders, raised his character in his own eyes and in the eyes of his neighbors. Nor indeed was his soldiership justly a subject of derision. In every county there were elderly gentlemen who had seen service which was no child's play. One had been knighted by Charles the First, after the battle of Edgehill. Another still wore a patch over the scar which he had received at Naseby. A third had defended his old house till Fairfax had blown in the door with a petard. The presence of these old Cavaliers, with their old swords and holsters, and with their old stories about Goring and Lunsford, gave to the musters of militia an earnest and warlike aspect which would otherwise have been wanting. Even those country gentlemen who were too young to have themselves ex-

England under the Restoration

changed blows with the cuirassiers of the Parliament had, from childhood, been surrounded by the traces of recent war, and fed with stories of the martial exploits of their fathers and uncles. Thus the character of the English esquire of the seventeenth century was compounded of two elements which we seldom or never find united. His ignorance and uncouthness, his low tastes and gross phrases, would, in our time, be considered as indicating a nature and a breeding thoroughly plebeian. Yet he was essentially a patrician, and had, in large measure, both the virtues and the vices which flourish among men set from their birth in high place, and used to respect themselves and to be respected by others. It is not easy for a generation accustomed to find chivalrous sentiments only in company with liberal studies and polished manners to image to itself a man with the deportment, the vocabulary, and the accent of a carter, yet punctilious on matters of genealogy and precedence, and ready to risk his life rather than see a stain cast on the honor of his house. It is however only by thus joining together things seldom or never found together in our own experience, that we can form a just idea of that rustic aristocracy which constituted the main strength of

England under the Restoration

the armies of Charles the First, and which long supported, with strange fidelity, the interest of his descendants.

The gross, uneducated, untraveled country gentleman was commonly a Tory; but, though devotedly attached to hereditary monarchy, he had no partiality for courtiers and ministers. He thought, not without reason, that Whitehall was filled with the most corrupt of mankind, and that of the great sums which the House of Commons had voted to the crown since the Restoration part had been embezzled by cunning politicians and part squandered on buffoons and foreign courtesans. His stout English heart swelled with indignation at the thought that the government of his country should be subject to French dictation. Being himself generally an old Cavalier, or the son of an old Cavalier, he reflected with bitter resentment on the ingratitude with which the Stuarts had requited their best friends. Those who heard him grumble at the neglect with which he was treated, and at the profusion with which wealth was lavished on the bastards of Nell Gwynn and Madam Carwell, would have supposed him ripe for rebellion. But all this ill humor lasted only till the throne was really in danger. It was precisely when those whom the sov-

England under the Restoration

ereign had loaded with wealth and honors shrank from his side that the country gentlemen, so surly and mutinous in the season of his prosperity, rallied round him in a body. Thus, after murmuring twenty years at the misgovernment of Charles the Second, they came to his rescue in his extremity, when his own Secretaries of State and the Lords of his own Treasury had deserted him, and enabled him to gain a complete victory over the opposition; nor can there be any doubt that they would have shown equal loyalty to his brother James if James would, even at the last moment, have refrained from outraging their strongest feeling. For there was one institution, and one only, which they prized even more than hereditary monarchy; and that institution was the Church of England. Their love of the Church was not, indeed, the effect of study or meditation. Few among them could have given any reason, drawn from Scripture or ecclesiastical history, for adhering to her doctrines, her ritual, and her polity; nor were they, as a class, by any means strict observers of that code of morality which is common to all Christian sects. But the experience of many ages proves that men may be ready to fight to the death, and to persecute without pity, for a religion whose creed they do not understand, and whose precepts they habitually disobey.*

Polite Literature

Good Latin scholars were numerous. The language of Rome, indeed, had not altogether lost its imperial prerogatives, and was still, in many parts of Europe, almost indispensable to a traveler or a negotiator. To speak it well was therefore a much more common accomplishment than in our time ; and neither Oxford nor Cambridge wanted poets who, on a great occasion, could lay at the foot of the throne happy imitations of the verses in which Virgil and Ovid had celebrated the greatness of Augustus.

Yet even the Latin was giving way to a younger rival. France united at that time almost every species of ascendency. Her military glory was at the height. She had vanquished mighty coalitions. She had dictated treaties. She had subjugated great cities and provinces. She had forced the Castilian pride to yield her the precedence. She had

---

* My notion of the country gentlemen of the seventeenth century has been derived from sources too numerous to be recapitulated. I must leave my description to the judgment of those who have studied the history and the lighter literature of that age.

England under the Restoration

summoned Italian princes to prostrate themselves at her footstool. Her authority was supreme in all matters of good breeding, from a duel to a minuet. She determined how a gentleman's coat must be cut, how long his peruke must be, whether his heels must be high or low, and whether the lace on his hat must be broad or narrow. In literature she gave law to the world. The fame of her great writers filled Europe. No other country could produce a tragic poet equal to Racine, a comic poet equal to Molière, a trifler so agreeable as La Fontaine, a rhetorician so skilful as Bossuet. The literary glory of Italy and of Spain had set; that of Germany had not yet dawned. The genius, therefore, of the eminent men who adorned Paris shone forth with a splendor which was set off to full advantage by contrast. France, indeed, had at that time an empire over mankind, such as even the Roman Republic never attained. For, when Rome was politically dominant, she was in arts and letters the humble pupil of Greece. France had, over the surrounding countries, at once the ascendency which Rome had over Greece, and the ascendency which Greece had over Rome. French was fast becoming the universal language, the language of fashionable society, the language of diplomacy. At

England under the Restoration

several courts princes and nobles spoke it more accurately and politely than their mother tongue. In our island there was less of this servility than on the Continent. Neither our good nor our bad qualities were those of imitators. Yet even here homage was paid, awkwardly indeed and sullenly, to the literary supremacy of our neighbors. The melodious Tuscan, so familiar to the gallants and ladies of the court of Elizabeth, sank into contempt. A gentleman who quoted Horace or Terence was considered in good company as a pompous pedant. But to garnish his conversation with scraps of French was the best proof which he could give of his parts and attainments.* New canons of criticism, new models of style came into fashion, The quaint ingenuity which had deformed the verses of Donne, and had been a blemish on those of Cowley, disappeared from our poetry. Our prose became less majestic, less artfully involved, less variously musical than that of an earlier age, but more lucid, more easy, and better fitted for controversy and narrative.

* Butler, in a satire of great asperity, says,

> " For, though to smatter words of Greek
> And Latin be the rhetorique
> Of pedants courted and vainglorious,
> To smatter French is meritorious."

England under the Restoration

In these changes it is impossible not to recognize the influence of French precept and of French example. Great masters of our language, in their most dignified compositions, affected to use French words, when English words, quite as expressive and sonorous, were at hand : * and from France was imported the tragedy in rhyme, an exotic which, in our soil, drooped, and speedily died.

It would have been well if our writers had also copied the decorum which their great French contemporaries, with few exceptions, preserved ; for the profligacy of the English plays, satires, songs, and novels of that age is a deep blot on our national fame. The evil may easily be traced to its source. The wits and the Puritans had never been on friendly terms. There was no sympathy between the two classes. They looked on the whole system of human life from different points and in different lights. The earnest of each was the jest of the other. The pleasures of each were the torments of the other. To the stern pre-

---

* The most offensive instance which I remember is in a poem on the coronation of Charles the Second by Dryden, who certainly could not plead poverty as an excuse for borrowing words from any foreign tougue :—

" Hither in summer evenings you repair
To taste the fraicheur of the cooler air."

England under the Restoration

cisian even the innocent sport of the fancy seemed a crime. To light and festive natures the solemnity of the zealous brethren furnished copious matter of ridicule. From the Reformation to the civil war, almost every writer, gifted with a fine sense of the ludicrous, had taken some opportunity of assailing the straight-haired, snuffling, whining saints, who christened their children out of the Book of Nehemiah, who groaned in spirit at the sight of Jack in the Green, and who thought it impious to taste plum porridge on Christmas day. At length a time came when the laughers began to look grave in their turn. The rigid, ungainly zealots, after having furnished much good sport during two generations, rose up in arms, conquered, ruled, and, grimly smiling, trod down under their feet the whole crowd of mockers. The wounds inflicted by gay and petulant malice were retaliated with the gloomy and implacable malice peculiar to bigots who mistake their own rancor for virtue. The theatres were closed, The players were flogged. The press was put under the guardianship of austere licensers. The Muses were banished from their own favorite haunts, Cambridge and Oxford. Cowley, Crashaw, and Cleveland were ejected from their fellowships. The

England under the Restoration

young candidate for academical honors was no longer required to write Ovidian epistles or Virgilian pastorals, but was strictly interrogated by a synod of lowering Supralapsarians as to the day and hour when he expreienced the new birth. Such a system was of course fruitful of hypocrites. Under sober clothing and under visages composed to the expression of austerity, lay hid during several years the intense desire of license and of revenge. At length that desire was gratified. The Restoration emancipated thousands of minds from a yoke which had become insupportable. The old fight recommenced, but with an animosity altogether new. It was now not a sportive combat, but a war to the death. The Roundhead had no better quarter to expect from those whom he had persecuted than a cruel slave-driver can expect from insurgent slaves still bearing the marks of his collars and his scourges.

The war between wit and Puritanism soon became a war between wit and morality. The hostility excited by a grotesque caricature of virtue did not spare virtue herself. Whatever the canting Roundhead had regarded with reverence was insulted. Whatever he had proscribed was favored. Because he had been scrupulous about trifles, all scruples

England under the Restoration

were treated with derision. Because he had covered his failings with the mask of devotion, men were encouraged to obtrude with Cynic impudence all their most scandalous vices on the public eye. Because he had punished illicit love with barbarous severity, virgin purity and conjugal fidelity were made a jest. To that sanctimonious jargon which was his Shibboleth, was opposed another jargon not less absurd and much more odious. As he never opened his mouth except in Scriptural phrase, the new breed of wits and fine gentlemen never opened their mouths without uttering ribaldry of which a porter would now be ashamed, and without calling on their Maker to curse them, sink them, confound them, blast them, and damn them.

It is not strange, therefore, that our polite literature, when it revived with the revival of the old civil and ecclesiastical polity, should have been profoundly immoral. A few eminent men, who belonged to an earlier and better age, were exempt from the general contagion. The verse of Waller still breathed the sentiments which had animated a more chivalrous generation. Cowley, distinguished as a loyalist and as a man of letters, raised his voice courageously against the immorality which disgraced both letters and loyalty. A

England under the Restoration

mightier poet, tried at once by pain, danger, poverty, obloquy, and blindness, meditated, undisturbed by the obscene tumult which raged all around him, a song so sublime and so holy that it would not have misbecome the lips of those ethereal Virtues whom he saw, with that inner eye which no calamity could darken, flinging down on the jasper pavement their crowns of amaranth and gold. The vigorous and fertile genius of Butler, if it did not altogether escape the prevailing infection, took the disease in a mild form. But these were men whose minds had been trained in a world which had passed away. They gave place in no long time to a younger generation of wits; and of that generation, from Dryden down to Durfey, the common characteristic was hardhearted, shameless, swaggering licentiousness, at once inelegant and inhuman. The influence of these writers was doubtless noxious, yet less noxious than it would have been had they been less depraved. The poison which they administered was so strong that it was, in no long time, rejected with nausea. None of them understood the dangerous art of associating images of unlawful pleasure with all that is endearing and ennobling. None of them was aware that a certain decorum is essential even to voluptuousness, that drapery

England under the Restoration

may be more alluring than exposure, and that the imagination may be far more powerfully moved by delicate hints which impel it to exert itself, than by gross descriptions which it takes impassively.

The spirit of the Anti-puritan reaction pervades almost the whole polite literature of the reign of Charles the Second. But the very quintessence of that spirit will be found in the comic drama. The playhouses, shut by the meddling fanatic in the day of his power, were again crowded. To their old attractions new and more powerful attractions had been added. Scenery, dresses, and decorations, such as would now be thought mean or absurd, but such as would have been esteemed incredibly magnificent by those who, early in the seventeenth century, sate on the filthy benches of the Hope, or under the thatched roof of the Rose, dazzled the eyes of the multitude. The fascination of sex was called in to aid the fascination of art : and the young spectator saw, with emotions unknown to the contemporaries of Shakspeare and Johnson, tender and sprightly heroines personated by lovely women. From the day on which the theatres were reopened they became seminaries of vice ; and the evil propagated itself. The profligacy of the representations soon drove away sober

England under the Restoration

people. The frivolous and dissolute who remained required every year stronger and stronger stimulants. Thus the artists corrupted the spectators, and the spectators the artists, till the turpitude of the drama became such as must astonish all who are not aware that extreme relaxation is the natural effect of extreme restraint, and that an age of hypocrisy is, in the regular course of things, followed by an age of impudence.

Nothing is more characteristic of the times than the care with which the poets contrived to put all their loosest verses into the mouths of women. The compositions in which the greatest license was taken were the epilogues. They were almost always recited by favorite actresses; and nothing charmed the depraved audience so much as to hear lines grossly indecent repeated by a beautiful girl, who was supposed to have not yet lost her innocence.*

Our theatre was indebted in that age for many plots and characters to Spain, to France, and to the old English masters: but whatever our dramatists touched they tainted. In their imitations the houses of Calderon's stately and high-spirited Castilian gentlemen became sties of vice, Shakspeare's Viola a procuress,

---

* Jeremy Collier has censured this odious practise with his usual force and keenness.

England under the Restoration

Molière's Misanthrope a ravisher, Moliere's Agnes an adulteress. Nothing could be so pure or so heroic but that it became foul and ignoble by transfusion through those foul and ignoble minds.

Such was the state of the drama; and the drama was the department of polite literature in which a poet had the best chance of obtaining a subsistence by his pen. The sale of books was so small that a man of the greatest name could hardly expect more than a pittance for the copyright of the best performance. There cannot be a stronger instance than the fate of Dryden's last production, the Fables. That volume was published when he was universally admitted to be the chief of living English poets. It contains about twelve thousand lines. The versification is admirable, the narratives and descriptions full of life. To this day Palamon and Arcite, Cymon and Iphigenia, Theodore and Honoria, are the delight both of critics and of schoolboys. The collection includes Alexander's Feast, the noblest ode in our language. For the copyright Dryden received two hundred and fifty pounds, less than in our days has sometimes been paid for two articles in a review.*

* The contrast will be found in Sir Walter Scott's edition of Dryden.

England under the Restoration

Nor does the bargain seem to have been a hard one. For the book went off slowly; and the second edition was not required till the author had been ten years in his grave. By writing for the theatre it was possible to earn a much larger sum with much less trouble. Southern made seven hundred pounds by one play.* Otway was raised from beggary to temporary affluence by the success of his Don Carlos.† Shadwell cleared a hundred and thirty pounds by a single representation of the Squire of Alsatia.‡ The consequence was that every man who had to live by his wit wrote plays, whether he had any internal vocation to write plays or not. It was thus with Dryden. As a satirist he has rivaled Juvenal. As a didactic poet he perhaps might, with care and meditation, have rivaled Lucretius. Of lyric poets he is, if not the most sublime, the most brilliant and spirit-stirring. But nature, profuse to him of many rare gifts, had withheld from him the dramatic faculty. Nevertheless all the energies of his best years were wasted on dramatic composition. He had too much judgment not to be aware that in the power of exhibiting character by means

---

* See the Life of Southern, by Shiels.
† See Rochester's Trial of the Poets.
‡ Some Account of the English Stage.

England under the Restoration

of dialogue he was deficient. That deficiency he did his best to conceal, sometimes by surprising and amusing incidents, sometimes by stately declamation, sometimes by harmonious numbers, sometimes by ribaldry but too well suited to the taste of a profane and licentious pit. Yet he never obtained any theatrical success equal to that which rewarded the exertions of some men far inferior to him in general powers. He thought himself fortunate if he cleared a hundred guineas by a play; a scanty remuneration, yet apparently larger than he could have earned in any other way by the same quantity of labor.*

The recompense which the wits of that age could obtain from the public was so small, that they were under the necessity of eking out their incomes by levying contributions on the great. Every rich and good-natured lord was pestered by authors with a mendicancy so importunate, and a flattery so abject, as may in our time seem incredible. The patron to whom a work was inscribed was expected to reward the writer with a purse of gold. The fee paid for the dedication of a book was often much larger than the sum which any publisher would give for the copyright. Books were therefore frequently printed merely that

* Life of Southern, by Shields.

England under the Restoration

they might be dedicated. This traffic in praise produced the effect which might have been expected. Adulation pushed to the verge, sometimes of nonsense, and sometimes of impiety, was not thought to disgrace a poet. Independence, veracity, self-respect, were things not required by the world from him. In truth, he was in morals something between a pandar and a beggar.

The Death of Charles II

From the "History of England," Chapter IV.

THE death of King Charles the Second took the nation by surprise. His frame was naturally strong, and did not appear to have suffered from excess. He had always been mindful of his health even in his pleasures; and his habits were such as promised a long life and a robust old age. Indolent as he was on all occasions which required tension of the mind, he was active and persevering in bodily exercise. He had, when young, been renowned as a tennis player,* and was, even in the decline of life, an indefatigable walker. His ordinary pace was such that those who were admitted to the honor of his society found it difficult to keep up with him. He rose early, and generally passed three or four hours a day in the open air. He might be seen, before the dew was off the grass in St. James's Park, striding among the trees, playing with his spaniels, and flinging corn to his ducks; and these exhibitions endeared him to the common

---
* Pepys's Diary, Dec 28, 1663, Sept. 2, 1667.

The Death of Charles II

people, who always love to see the great unbend.*

At length, towards the close of the year 1684, he was prevented, by a slight attack of what was supposed to be gout, from rambling as usual. He now spent his mornings in his laboratory, where he amused himself with experiments on the properties of mercury. His temper seemed to have suffered from confinement. He had no apparent cause for disquiet. His kingdom was tranquil: he was not in pressing want of money: his power was greater than it had ever been: the party which had long thwarted him had been beaten down; but the cheerfulness which had supported him against adverse fortune had vanished in this season of prosperity. A trifle now sufficed to depress those elastic spirits which had borne up against defeat, exile, and penury. His irritation frequently showed itself by looks and words such as could hardly have been expected from a man so eminently distinguished by good humor and good breeding. It was not supposed however that his constitution was seriously impaired.†

His palace had seldom presented a gayer

† Burnet, i. 606; Spectator, No. 462; Lords' Journals, October 28, 1678; Cibber's Apology.

* Burnet, i. 605, 606; Welwood; North's Life of Guildford, 251.

The Death of Charles II

or a more scandalous appearance than on the evening of Sunday the first of February 1685.* Some grave persons who had gone thither, after the fashion of that age, to pay their duty to their sovereign, and who had expected that, on such a day, his court would wear a decent aspect, were struck with astonishment and horror. The great gallery of Whitehall, an admirable relic of the magnificence of the Tudors, was crowded with revelers and gamblers. The king sate there chatting and toying with three women, whose charms were the boast, and whose vices were the disgrace, of three nations. Barbara Palmer, Duchess of Cleveland, was there, no longer young, but still retaining some traces of that superb and voluptuous loveliness which twenty years before overcame the hearts of all men. There too was the Duchess of Portsmouth, whose soft and infantine features were lighted up with the vivacity of France. Hortensia Mancini, Duchess of Mazarin, and niece of the great Cardinal, completed the group. She had been early removed from her native Italy to the court where her uncle was supreme. His power and her own attractions had drawn

* I may take this opportunity of mentioning that whenever I give only one date, I follow the old style, which was, in the seventeenth century, the style of England; but I reckon the year from the first of January.

The Death of Charles II

a crowd of illustrious suitors round her. Charles himself, during his exile, had sought her hand in vain. No gift of nature or of fortune seemed to be wanting to her. Her face was beautiful with the rich beauty of the South, her understanding quick, her manners graceful, her rank exalted, her possessions immense ; but her ungovernable passions had turned all these blessings into curses. She had found the misery of an ill-assorted marriage intolerable, had fled from her husband, had abandoned her vast wealth, and, after having astonished Rome and Piedmont by her adventures, had fixed her abode in England. Her house was the favorite resort of men of wit and pleasure, who, for the sake of her smiles and her table, endured her frequent fits of insolence and ill-humor. Rochester and Godolphin semetimes forgot the cares of state in her company. Barillon and Saint Evremond found in her drawing-room consolation for their long banishment from Paris. The learning of Vossius, the wit of Waller, were daily employed to flatter and amuse her. But her diseased mind required stronger stimulants, and sought them in gallantry, in basset, and in usquebaugh.* While Charles flirted with

---

* Saint Evremond, *passim* ; Saint Réal, Mémoires de la Duchesse de Mazarin ; Rochester's Farewell; Evelyn's Diary, Sept. 6, 1676, June 11, 169.

The Death of Charles II

his three sultanas, Hortensia's French page, a handsome boy, whose vocal performances were the delight of Whitehall, and were rewarded by numerous presents of rich clothes, ponies, and guineas, warbled some amorous verses.* A party of twenty courtiers was seated at cards round a large table on which gold was heaped in mountains.† Even then the King had complained that he did not feel quite well. He had no appetite for his supper: his rest that night was broken; but on the following morning he rose, as usual, early.

To that morning the contending factions in his council had, during some days, looked forward with anxiety. The struggle between Halifax and Rochester seemed to be approaching a decisive crisis. Halifax, not content with having already driven his rival from the Board of Treasury, had undertaken to prove him guilty of such dishonesty or neglect in the conduct of the finances as ought to be punished by dismission from the public service. It was even whispered that the Lord President would probably be sent to the Tower. The King had promised to inquire into the matter. The second of February had been fixed for the

* Evelyn's Diary, Jan. 28, 1684-5; Saint Evremond's Letter to Déry.
† Id., February 4, 1684-5.

The Death of Charles II

investigation ; and several officers of the revenue had been ordered to attend with their books on that day.* But a great turn of fortune was at hand.

Scarcely had Charles risen from his bed when his attendants perceived that his utterance was indistinct, and that his thoughts seemed to be wandering. Several men of rank had, as usual, assembled to see their sovereign shaved and dressed. He made an effort to converse with them in his usual gay style ; but his ghastly look surprised and alarmed them. Soon his face grew black ; his eyes turned in his head ; he uttered a cry, staggered, and fell into the arms of one of his lords. A physician who had charge of the royal retorts and crucibles happened to be present. He had no lancet ; but he opened a vein with a penknife. The blood flowed freely ; but the King was still insensible.

He was laid on his bed, where, during a short time, the Duchess of Portsmouth hung over him with the familiarity of a wife. But the alarm had been given. The Queen and the Duchess of York were hastening to the room.

---

* Roger North's Life of Sir Dudley North, 170· The true Patriot vindicated, or a Justification of his Excellency the E—— of R——; Burnet, i. 605. The Treasury Books prove that Burnet had good intelligence.

The Death of Charles II

'The favorite concubine was forced to retire to her own apartments. Those apartments had been thrice pulled down and thrice rebuilt by her lover to gratify her caprice. The very furniture of the chimney was massy silver. Several fine paintings, which properly belonged to the Queen, had been transferred to the dwelling of the mistress. The sideboards were piled with richly wrought plate. In the niches stood cabinets, the masterpieces of Japanese art. On the hangings, fresh from the looms of Paris, were depicted, in tints which no English tapestry could rival, birds of gorgeous plumage, landscapes, hunting matches, the lordly terrace of Saint Germains, the statues and fountains of Versailles.* In the midst of this splendor, purchased by guilt and shame, the unhappy woman gave herself up to an agony of grief, which, to do her justice, was not wholly selfish.

And now the gates of Whitehall, which ordinarily stood open to all comers, were closed. But persons whose faces were known were still permitted to enter. The antechambers and galleries were soon filled to overflowing; and even the sick room was crowded with peers, privy councilors, and foreign ministers. All the medical men of note in

* Evelyn's Diary, Jan. 24. 1681-2, Oct. 4, 1683.

The Death of Charles II

London were summoned. So high did political animosities run that the presence of some Whig physicians was regarded as an extraordinary circumstance.* One Roman Catholic, whose skill was then widely renowned, Doctor Thomas Short, was in attendance. Several of the prescriptions have been preserved. One of them is signed by fourteen Doctors. The patient was bled largely. Hot iron was applied to his head. A loathsome volatile salt, extracted from human skulls, was forced into his mouth. He recovered his senses; but he was evidently in a situation of extreme danger.

The Queen was for a time assiduous in her attendance. The Duke of York scarcely left his brother's bedside. The Primate and four other bishops were then in London. They remained at Whitehall all day, and took it by turns to sit up at night in the King's room. The news of his illness filled the capital with sorrow and dismay. For his easy temper and affable manners had won the affection of a large part of the nation; and those who most disliked him preferred his unprincipled levity to the stern and earnest bigotry of his brother.

On the morning of Thursday the fifth of February, the London Gazette announced that

* Dugdale's Correspondence.

The Death of Charles II

His Majesty was going on well, and was thought by the physicians to be out of danger. The bells of all the churches rang merrily; and preparations for bonfires were made in the streets. But in the evening it was known that a relapse had taken place, and that the medical attendants had given up all hope. The public mind was greatly disturbed; but there was no disposition to tumult. The Duke of York, who had already taken on himself to give orders, ascertained that the City was perfectly quiet, and that he might without difficulty be proclaimed as soon as his brother should expire.

The King was in great pain, and complained that he felt as if a fire was burning within him. Yet he bore up against his sufferings with a fortitude which did not seem to belong to his soft and luxurious nature. The sight of his misery affected his wife so much that she fainted, and was carried senseless to her chamber. The prelates who were in waiting had from the first exhorted him to prepare for his end. They now thought it their duty to address him in a still more urgent manner. William Sancroft, Archbishop of Canterbury, an honest and pious, though narrow-minded, man, used great freedom. "It is time," he said, "to speak out; for, Sir, you are about

The Death of Charles II

to appear before a Judge who is no respecter of persons." The King answered not a word.

Thomas Ken, Bishop of Bath and Wells, then tried his powers of persuasion. He was a man of parts and learning, of quick sensibility and stainless virtue. His elaborate works have long been forgotten; but his morning and evening hymns are still repeated daily in thousands of dwellings. Though like most of his order, zealous for monarchy, he was no sycophant. Before he became a Bishop, he had maintained the honor of his gown by refusing, when the court was at Winchester, to let Eleanor Gwynn lodge in the house which he occupied there as a prebendary.* The King had sense enough to respect so manly a spirit. Of all the prelates he liked Ken the best. It was to no purpose, however, that the good Bishop now put forth all his eloquence. His solemn and pathetic exhortation awed and melted the bystanders to such a degree that some among them believed him to be filled with the same spirit which, in the old time, had, by the mouths of Nathan and Elias, called sinful princes to repentance. Charles however was unmoved. He made no objection indeed when the service for the visi-

* Hawkins's Life of Ken, 1713.

The Death of Charles II

tation of the sick was read. In reply to the pressing questions of the divines, he said that he was sorry for what he had done amiss; and he suffered the absolution to be pronounced over him according to the forms of the Church of England: but, when he was urged to declare that he died in the communion of that Church, he seemed not to hear what was said; and nothing could induce him to take the Eucharist from the hands of the Bishops. A table with bread and wine was brought to his bedside, but in vain. Sometimes he said that there was no hurry, and sometimes that he was too weak.

Many attributed this apathy to contempt for divine things, and many to the stupor which often precedes death. But there were in the palace a few persons who knew better. Charles had never been a sincere member of the Established Church. His mind had long oscillated between Hobbism and Popery. When his health was good and his spirits high he was a scoffer. In his few serious moments he was a Roman Catholic. The Duke of York was aware of this, but was entirely occupied with the care of his own interests. He had ordered the outports to be closed. He had posted detachments of the Guards in different parts of the city. He had also pro-

The Death of Charles II

cured the feeble signature of the dying King to an instrument by which some duties, granted only till the demise of the Crown, were let to farm for a term of three years. These things occupied the attention of James to such a degree that, though, on ordinary occasions, he was indiscreetly and unseasonably eager to bring over proselytes to his Church, he never reflected that his brother was in danger of dying without the last sacraments. This neglect was the more extraordinary because the Duchess of York had, at the request of the Queen, suggested, on the morning on which the King was taken ill, the propriety of procuring spiritual assistance. For such assistance Charles was at last indebted to an agency very different from that of his pious wife and sister-in-law. A life of frivolity and vice had not extinguished in the Duchess of Portsmouth all sentiments of religion, or all that kindness which is the glory of her sex. The French ambassador Barillon, who had come to the palace to inquire after the King, paid her a visit. He found her in an agony of sorrow. She took him into a secret room, and poured out her whole heart to him. "I have," she said, "a thing of great moment to tell you. If it were known my head would be in danger. The King is really and truly a Catholic; but

The Death of Charles II

he will die without being reconciled to the Church. His bedchamber is full of Protestant clergymen. I cannot enter it without giving scandal. The Duke is thinking only of himself. Speak to him. Remind him that there is a soul at stake. He is master now. He can clear the room. Go this instant, or it will be too late."

Barillon hastened to the bedchamber, took the Duke aside, and delivered the message of the mistress. The conscience of James smote him. He started as if roused from sleep, and declared that nothing should prevent him from discharging the sacred duty which had been too long delayed. Several schemes were discussed and rejected. At last the Duke commanded the crowd to stand aloof, went to the bed, stooped down, and whispered something which none of the spectators could hear, but which they supposed to be some question about affairs of state. Charles answered in an audible voice, "Yes, yes, with all my heart." None of the bystanders, except the French Ambassador, guessed that the King was declaring his wish to be admitted into the bosom of the Church of Rome.

"Shall I bring a priest?" said the Duke. "Do, brother," replied the sick man. "For

The Death of Charles II

God's sake do, and lose no time. But no; you will get into trouble." "If it costs me my life," said the Duke, "I will fetch a priest."

To find a priest, however, for such a purpose, at a moment's notice, was not easy. For, as the law then stood, the person who admitted a proselyte into the Roman Catholic Church was guilty of a capital crime. The Count of Castel Melhor, a Portuguese nobleman, who, driven by political troubles from his native land, had been hospitably received at the English court, undertook to procure a confessor. He had recourse to his countrymen who belonged to the Queen's household; but he found that none of her chaplains knew English or French enough to shrive the King. The Duke and Barillon were about to send to the Venetian Minister for a clergyman when they heard that a Benedictine monk, named John Huddleston, happened to be at Whitehall. This man had, with great risk to himself, saved the King's life after the battle of Worcester, and had, on that account, been, ever since the Restoration, a privileged person. In the sharpest proclamations which had been put forth against Popish priests, when false witnesses had inflamed the nation to fury, Huddleston had

The Death of Charles II

been excepted by name.* He readily consented to put his life a second time in peril for his prince; but there was still a difficulty. The honest monk was so illiterate that he did not know what he ought to say on an occasion of such importance. He however obtained some hints, through the intervention of Castel Melhar, from a Portuguese ecclesiastic, and, thus instructed, was brought up the back stairs by Chiffinch, a confidential servant, who, if the satires of that age are to be credited, had often introduced visitors of a very different description by the same entrance. The Duke then, in the King's name, commanded all who were present to quit the room, except Lewis Duras, Earl of Feversham, and John Granville, Earl of Bath. Both these Lords professed the Protestant religion; but James conceived that he could count on their fidelity. Feversham, a Frenchman of noble birth, and nephew of the great Turenne, held high rank in the English army, and was Chamberlain to the Queen. Bath was Groom of the Stole.

The Duke's orders were obeyed; and even the physicians withdrew. The back door

---

* See the London Gazette of Nov. 21, 1678. Barillon and Burnet say that Huddleston was excepted out of all the Acts of Parliament made against priests; but this is a mistake.

The Death of Charles II

was then opened; and Father Huddleston entered. A cloak had been thrown over his sacred vestments; and his shaven crown was concealed by a flowing wig. "Sir," said the Duke, "this good man once saved your life. He now comes to save your soul." Charles faintly answered, "He is welcome." Huddleston went through his part better than had been expected. He knelt by the bed, listened to the confession, pronounced the absolution, and administered extreme unction. He asked if the King wished to receive the Lord's supper, "Surely," said Charles, "if I am not unworthy." The host was brought in Charles feebly strove to rise and kneel before it. The priest made him lie still, and assured him that God would accept the humiliation of the soul, and would not require the humiliation of the body. The King found so much difficulty in swallowing the bread that it was necessary to open the door and procure a glass of water. This rite ended, the monk held up a crucifix before the penitent, charged him to fix his last thoughts on the sufferings of the Redeemer, and withdrew. The whole ceremony had occupied about three quarters of an hour; and, during that time, the courtiers who filled the outer room had communicated their suspicions to each other

The Death of Charles II

by whispers and significant glances. The door was at length thrown open, and the crowd again filled the chamber of death.

It was now late in the evening. The King seemed much relieved by what had passed. His natural children were brought to his bedside, the Dukes of Grafton, Southampton, and Northumberland, sons of the Duchess of Cleveland, the Duke of Saint Albans, son of Eleanor Gwynn, and the Duke of Richmond, son of the Duchess of Portsmouth. Charles blessed them all, but spoke with peculiar tenderness to Richmond. One face which should have been there was wanting. The eldest and best loved child was an exile and a wanderer. His name was not once mentioned by his father.

During the night Charles earnestly recommended the Duchess of Portsmouth and her boy to the care of James; "And do not," he good-naturedly added, " let poor Nelly starve." The Queen sent excuses for her absence by Halifax. She said that she was too much disordered to resume her post by the couch, and implored pardon for any offense which she might unwittingly have given. "She ask my pardon, poor woman!" cried Charles; "I ask hers with all my heart."

The morning light began to peep through

The Death of Charles II

the windows of Whitehall; and Charles desired the attendants to pull aside the curtains, that he might have one more look at the day. He remarked that it was time to wind up a clock which stood near his bed. These little circumstances were long remembered because they proved beyond dispute that, when he declared himself a Roman Catholic, he was in full possession of his faculties. He apologized to those who had stood round him all night for the trouble which he had caused. He had been, he said, a most unconscionable time dying; but he hoped that they would excuse it. This was the last glimpse of the exquisite urbanity, so often found potent to charm away the resentment of a justly incensed nation. Soon after dawn the speech of the dying man failed. Before ten his senses were gone. Great numbers had repaired to the churches at the hour of morning service. When the prayer for the King was read, loud groans and sobs showed how deeply his people felt for him. At noon on Friday, the sixth of February, he passed away without a struggle.*

* Clark's Life of James the Second, 1. 746. Orig. Mem.; Barillon's Despatch of Feb. 1-18, 1685; Van Citters's Despatches of Feb. 3-13 and Feb. 6-16. Huddleston's Narrative; Letters of

The Death of Charles II

Philip, second Earl of Chesterfield, 277; Sir H. Ellis's Original Letters, First Series, iii. 333; Second Series iv. 74; Chaillot MS.; Burnet, i. 606; Evelyn's Diary, Feb. 4, 1684-5; Welwood's Memories, 140; North's Life of Guildford, 252; Examen, 648; Hawkins's Life of Ken; Dryden's Threnodia Augustalis; Sir H. Halford's Essay on Deaths of Eminent Persons. See also a fragment of a letter written by the Earl of Ailesbury, which is printed in the European Magazine for April, 1705. Atlesbury calls Burnet an impostor. Yet his own narrative and Burnet's will not, to any candid and sensible reader, appear to contradict each other. I have seen in the British Museum, and also in the Library of the Royal Institution, a curious broadside containing an account of the death of Charles. It will be found in the Somers Collections. The author was evidently a zealous Roman Catholic, and must have had access to good sources of information. I strongly suspect that he had been in communication, directly or indirectly, with James himself. No name is given at length; but the initials are perfectly intelligible, except in one place. It is said that the D. of Y. was reminded of the duty which he owed to his brother by P. M. A. C. F. I must own myself quite unable to decipher the last five letters. It is some consolation that Sir Walter Scott was equally unsuccessful. (1848.) Since the first edition of this work was published, several ingenious conjectures touching these mysterious letters have been communicated to me; but I am convinced that the true solution has not yet been suggested. (1850.) I still greatly doubt whether the riddle has been solved. But the most plausible interpretation is one which, with some variations, occurred, almost at the same time, to myself and to several other persons; I am inclined to read "Pere Mansuete, A Cordelier Friar." Mansuete, a Cordelier, was then James's confessor. To Mansuete therefore it peculiarly belonged to remind James of a sacred duty which had been culpably neglected. The writer of the broadside must have been unwilling to inform the world that a soul which many devout Roman Catholics had left to perish had been snatched from destruction by the courageous charity of a woman of loose character. It is therefore not unlikely that he would prefer a fiction, at once probable and edifying, to a truth which could not fail to give scandal. (1856).

The Death of Charles II

It should seem that no transactions in history ought to be more accurately known to us than those which took place round the deathbed of Charles the Second. We have several relations written by persons who were actually in his room. We have several relations written by persons who, though not themselves eye-witnesses, had the best opportunity of obtaining information from eye-witnesses. Yet whoever attempts to digest this vast mass of materials into a consistent narrative will find the task a difficult one. Indeed James and his wife, when they told the story to the nuns of Chaillot, could not agree as to some circumstances. The Queen said that, after Charles had received the last sacraments the Protestant Bishops renewed their exhortations. The King said that nothing of the kind took place. "Surely," said the Queen, "you told me so yourself." "It is impossible that I could have told you so," said the King; "for nothing of the sort happened."

The Revolution of 1688

From the "History of England," Chapter X.

THUS was consummated the English Revolution. When we compare it with those revolutions which have, during the last sixty years, overthrown so many ancient governments, we cannot but be struck by its peculiar character. Why that character was so peculiar is sufficiently obvious, and yet seems not to have been always understood either by eulogists or by censors.

The Continental revolutions of the eighteenth and nineteenth centuries took place in countries where all trace of the limited monarchy of the middle ages had long been effaced. The right of the prince to make laws and to levy money had, during many generations, been undisputed. His throne was guarded by a great regular army. His administration could not, without extreme peril, be blamed even in the mildest terms. His subjects held their personal liberty by no other tenure than his pleasure. Not a single institution was left which had within the

The Revolution of 1688

memory of the oldest man, afforded efficient protection to the subject against the utmost excess of tyranny. Those great councils which had once curbed the regal power had sunk into oblivion. Their composition and their privileges were known only to antiquaries. We cannot wonder, therefore, that when men who had been thus ruled succeeded in wresting supreme power from a government which they had long in secret hated, they should have been impatient to demolish and unable to construct, that they should have been fascinated by every specious novelty, that they should have proscribed every title, ceremony, and phrase associated with the old system, and that, turning away with disgust from their own national precedents and traditions, they should have sought for principles of government in the writings of theorists, or aped, with ignorant and ungraceful affectation, the partiots of Athens and Rome. As little can we wonder that the violent action of the revolutionary spirit should have been followed by reaction equally violent, and that confusion should speedily have engendered despotism sterner than that from which it had sprung.

Had we been in the same situation; had Strafford succeeded in his favorite scheme of Thorough; had he formed an army as

The Revolution of 1688

numerous and as well disciplined as that which, a few years later, was formed by Cromwell; had a series of judicial decisions, similar to that which was pronounced by the Exchequer Chamber in the case of ship money transferred to the crown the right of taxing the people; had the Star Chamber and the High Commission continued to fine, mutilate, and imprison every man who dared to raise his voice against the government; had the press been as completely enslaved here as at Vienna or at Naples; had our Kings gradually drawn to themselves the whole legislative power; had six generations of Englishmen passed away without a single session of Parliament; and had we then at length risen up in some moment of wild excitement against our masters, what an outbreak would that have been! With what a crash, heard and felt to the farthest end of the world, would the whole vast fabric of society have fallen! How many thousands of exiles, once the most prosperous and the most refined members of this great community, would have begged their bread in Continental cities, or have sheltered their heads under huts of bark in the uncleared forests of America! How often should we have seen the pavement of London piled up in barricades, the houses

The Revolution of 1688

dinted with bullets, the gutters foaming with blood! How many times should we have rushed widly from extreme to extreme, sought refuge from anarchy in despotism, and been again driven by despotism into anarchy! How many years of blood and confusion would it have cost us to learn the very rudiments of political science! How many childish theories would have duped us! How many rude and ill-poised constitutions should we have set up, only to see them tumble down! Happy would it have been for us if a sharp discipline of half a century had sufficed to educate us into a capacity of enjoying true freedom.

These calamities our Revolution averted. It was a revolution strictly defensive, and had prescription and legitimacy on its side. Here, and here only, a limited monarchy of the thirteenth century had come down unimpaired to the seventeenth century. Our parliamentary institutions were in full vigor. The main principles of our government were excellent. They were not, indeed, formally and exactly set forth in a single written instrument: but they were to be found scattered over our ancient and noble statutes; and, what was of far greater moment, they had been engraven on the hearts of Englishmen during four hundred years. That, without the consent of the rep-

The Revolution of 1688

resentatives of the nation, no legislative act could be passed, no tax imposed, no regular soldiery kept up, that no man could be imprisoned, even for a day, by the arbitrary will of the sovereign, that no tool of power could plead the royal command as a justification for violating any right of the humblest subject, were held both by Whigs and Tories, to be fundamental laws of the realm. A realm of which these were the fundamental laws stood in no need of a new constitution.

But, though a new constitution was not needed, it was plain that changes were required. The misgovernment of the Stuarts, and the troubles which that misgovernment had produced, sufficiently proved that there was somewhere a defect in our polity; and that defect it was the duty of the Convention to discover and to supply.

Some questions of great moment were still open to dispute. Our constitution had begun to exist in times when statesmen were not much accustomed to frame exact definitions. Anomalies, therefore, inconsistent with its principles and dangerous to its very existence, had sprung up almost imperceptibly, and, not having during many years caused any serious inconvenience, had gradually acquired the force of prescription. The remedy for these

The Revolution of 1688

evils was to assert the rights of the people in such a language as should terminate all controversy, and to declare that no precedent could justify any violation of those rights.

When this had been done it would be impossible for our rulers to misunderstand the law: but, unless something more were done, it was by no means improbable that they might violate it. Unhappily the Church had long taught the nation that hereditary monarchy, alone among our institutions, was divine and inviolable; that the right of the House of Commons to a share in the legislative power was a right merely human, but that the right of the King to the obedience of his people was from above; that the Great Charter was the statute which might be repealed by those who had made it, but that the rule which called the princes of the blood-royal to the throne in order of succession was of celestial origin, and that any Act of Parliament inconsistent with that rule was a nullity. It is evident that, in a society in which such superstitions prevail, constitutional freedom must ever be insecure. A power which is regarded merely as the ordinance of man cannot be an efficient check on a power which is regarded as the ordinance of God. It is vain to hope that laws, however excellent, will per-

The Revolution of 1688

manently restrain a king who, in his own opinion, and in the opinion of a great part of his people, has an authority infinitely higher in kind than the authority which belongs to those laws. To deprive royalty of these mysterious attributes, and to establish the principle that Kings reigned by a right in no respect differing from the right by which freeholders chose knights of the shire, or from the right by which Judges granted writs of Habeas Corpus, was absolutely necessary to the security of our liberties.

Thus the Convention had two great duties to perform. The first was to clear the fundamental laws of the realm from ambiguity. The second was to eradicate from the minds, both of the governors and of the governed, the false and pernicious notion that the royal prerogative was something more sublime and holy than those fundamental laws. The former object was attained by the solemn recital and claim with which the Declaration of Right commences ; the latter by the resolution which pronounced the throne vacant, and invited William and Mary to fill it.

The change seems small. Not a single flower of the crown was touched. Not a single new right was given to the people. The whole English law, substantive and adjective,

The Revolution of 1688

was, in the judgment of all the greatest lawyers, of Holt and Treby, of Maynard and Somers, almost exactly the same after the Revolution as before it. Some controverted points had been decided according to the sense of the best jurists : and there had been a slight deviation from the ordinary course of succession. This was all ; and this was enough.

As our Revolution was a vindication of ancient rights, so it was conducted with strict attention to ancient formalities. In almost every word and act may be discerned a profound reverence for the past. The Estates of the Realm deliberated in the old halls and according to the old rules. Powle was conducted to his chair between his mover and his seconder with the accustomed forms. The Sergeant with his mace brought up the messengers of the Lords to the table of the Commons ; and the three obeisances were duly made. The conference was held with all the antique ceremonial. On one side of the table, in the Painted Chamber, the managers for the Lords sat covered and robed in ermine and gold. The managers for the Commons stood bareheaded on the other side. The speeches present an almost ludicrous contrast to the revolutionary oratory of every other country. Both the English parties agreed in treating

The Revolution of 1688

with solemn respect the ancient constitutional traditions of the state. The only question was in what sense those traditions were to be understood. The assertors of liberty said not a word about the natural equality of men and the inalienable sovereignty of the people, about Harmodius or Timoleon, Brutus, the elder or Brutus the younger. When they were told that, by the English law, the crown, at the moment of a demise, must descend to the next heir, they answered that, by the English law, a living man could have no heir. When they were told that there was no precedent for declaring the throne vacant, they produced from among the records in the Tower a roll of parchment, near three hundred years old, on which, in quaint characters and barbarous Latin, it was recorded that the Estates of the Realm had declared vacant the throne of a perfidious and tyrannical Plantagenet. When at length the dispute had been accommodated, the new sovereigns were proclaimed with the old pageantry. All the fantastic pomp of heraldry was there, Clarencieux and Norroy, Portcullis and Rouge Dragon, the trumpets, the banners, the grotesque coats embroidered with lions and lilies. The title of King of France, assumed by the conqueror of Cressy, was not omitted in the royal style. To us,

The Revolution of 1688

who have lived in the year 1848, it may seem almost an abuse of terms to call a proceeding, conducted with so much deliberation, with so much sobriety, and with such minute attention to proscriptive etiquette, by the terrible name of Revolution.

And yet this revolution, of all revolutions the least violent, has been of all revolutions the most beneficent. It finally decided the great question whether the popular element which had, ever since the age of Fitzwalter and DeMontfort, been found in the English polity, should be destroyed by the monarchical element, or should be suffered to develop itself freely, and to become dominant. The strife between the two principles had been long, fierce, and doubtful. It had lasted through four reigns. It had produced seditions, impeachments, rebellions, battles, sieges, proscriptions, judicial massacres. Sometimes liberty, sometimes royalty, had seemed to be on the point of perishing. During many years one half of the energy of England had been employed in counteracting the other half. The executive power and the legislative power had so effectually impeded each other that the state had been of no account in Europe. The King at Arms, who proclaimed William and Mary before White-

The Revolution of 1688

hall Gate, did in truth announce that this great struggle was over; that there was entire union between the throne and the Parliament; that England, long dependent and degraded, was again a power of the first rank; that the ancient laws by which the prerogative was bounded would thenceforth be held as sacred as the prerogative itself, and would be followed out to all their consequences; that the executive administration would be conducted in conformity with the sense of the representatives of the nation; and that no reform, which the two Houses should, after mature deliberation, propose, would be obstinately withstood by the sovereign. The Declaration of Right, though it made nothing law which had not been law before, contained the germ of the law which gave religious freedom to the Dissenter, of the law which secured the independence of the judges, of the law which limited the duration of Parliaments, of the law which placed the liberty of the press under the protection of juries, of the law which prohibited the slave trade, of the law which abolished the sacramental test, of the law which relieved the Roman Catholics from civil disabilities, of the law which reformed the representative system, of every god law which has been passed during more than a century and a half,

The Revolution of 1688

of every good law which may hereafter, in the course of ages, be found necessary to promote the public weal, and to satisfy the demands of public opinion.

The highest eulogy which can be pronounced on the revolution of 1688 is this, that it was our last revolution. Several generations have now passed away since any wise and patriotic Englishman has meditated resistance to the established government. In all honest and reflecting minds there is a conviction, daily strengthened by experience, that the means of effecting every improvement which the constitution requires may be found within the constitution itself.

Now, if ever, we ought to be able to appreciate the whole importance of the stand which was made by our forefathers against the House of Stuart.* All around us the world is convulsed by the agonies of great nations. Governments which lately seemed likely to stand during ages have been on a sudden shaken and overthrown. The proudest Capitals of Western Europe have streamed with civil blood. All evil passions, the thirst of gain and the thirst of vengeance, the antipathy of class to class, the antipathy of race to race, have broken loose from the control

---

* This passage was written in November, 1848.

The Revolution of 1688

of divine and human laws. Fear and anxiety have clouded the faces and depressed the hearts of millions. Trade has been suspended and industry paralyzed. The rich have become poor; and the poor have become poorer. Doctrines hostile to all sciences, to all arts, to all industry, to all domestic charities, doctrines which, if carried into effect, would, in thirty years, undo all that thirty centuries have done for mankind, and would make the fairest provinces of France and Germany as savage as Congo or Patagonia, have been avowed from the tribune and defended by the sword. Europe has been threatened with subjugation by barbarians, compared with whom the barbarians who marched under Attila and Albion were enlightened and humane. The truest friends of the people have with deep sorrow owned that interests more precious than any political privileges were in jeopardy, and that it might be necessary to sacrifice even liberty in order to save civilization. Meanwhile in our island the regular course of government has never been for a day interrupted. The few bad men who longed for license and plunder have not had the courage to confront for one moment the strength of a loyal nation, rallied in firm array round a parental throne. And, if it be

The Revolution of 1688

asked what has made us to differ from others, the answer is that we never lost what others are wildly and blindly seeking to regain. It is because we had a preserving revolution in the seventeenth century that we have not had a destroying revolution in the nineteeth. It is because we had freedom in the midst of servitude that we have order in the midst of anarchy. For the authority of law, for the security of property, for the peace of our streets, for the happiness of our homes, our gratitude is due, under Him who raises and pulls down nations at his pleasure, to the Long Parliament, to the Convention, and to William of Orange.

The Origin of the National Debt

From the "History of England," Chapter XIX.

During the interval between the Restoration and the Revolution the riches of the nation had been rapidly increasing. Thousands of busy men found every Christmas that, after the expenses of the year's housekeeping had been defrayed out of the year's income, a surplus remained ; and how that surplus was to be employed was a question of some difficulty. In our time, to invest such a surplus, at something more than three per cent, on the best security that has ever been known in the world, is the work of a few minutes. But, in the seventeenth century, a lawyer, a physician. a retired merchant, who had saved some thousands and who wished to place them safely and profitably, was often greatly embarrassed. Three generations earlier, a man who had accumulated wealth in a trade or a profession generally purchased real property or lent his savings on mortgage. But the number of acres in the kingdom had remained the same ; and the value of those acres,

The Origin of the National Debt

though it had greatly increased, had by no means increased so fast as the quantity of capital which was seeking for employment. Many too wished to put their money where they could find it at an hour's notice, and looked about for some species of property which could be more readily transferred than a house or a field. A capitalist might lend on bottomry or on personal security: but, if he did so, he ran a great risk of losing interest and principal. There were a few joint stock companies, among which the East India Company held the foremost place; but the demand for the stock of such companies was far greater than the supply. Indeed the cry for a new East India Company was chiefly raised by persons who had found difficulty in placing their savings at interest on good security. So great was that difficulty that the practice of hoarding was common. We are told that the father of Pope, the poet, who retired from business in the City about the time of the Revolution, carried to a retreat in the country a strong box containing near twenty thousand pounds, and took out from time to time what was required for household expenses; and it is highly probable that this was not a solitary case. At present the quantity of coin which is hoarded by private persons is so

The Origin of the National Debt

small that it would, if brought forth, make no perceptible addition to the circulation. But, in the earlier part of the reign of William the Third, all the greatest writers on currency were of opinion that a very considerable mass of gold and silver was hidden in secret drawers and behind wainscots.

The natural effect of this state of things was that a crowd of projectors, ingenious and absurd, honest and knavish, employed themselves in devising new schemes for the employment of redundant capital. It was about the year 1688, that the word stockjobber was first heard in London, In the short space of four years a crowd of companies, every one of which confidently held out to subscribers the hope of immense gains, sprang into existence; the Insurance Company, the Paper Company, the Lutestring Company, the Pearl Fishery Company, the Glass Bottle Company, the Alum Company, the Blythe Coal Company, the Swordblade Company. There was a Tapestry Company, which would soon furnish pretty hangings for all the parlors of the middle class and for all the bedchambers of the higher. There was a Copper Company, which proposed to explore the mines of England, and held out a hope that they would prove not less valuable than those

The Origin of the National Debt

of Potosi. There was a Diving Company, which undertook to bring up precious effects from shipwrecked vessels, and which announced that it had laid in a stock of wonderful machines resembling complete suits of armor. In front of the helmet was a huge glass eye like that of Polyphemus; and out of the crest went a pipe through which the air was to be admitted. The whole process was exhibited on the Thames, Fine gentlemen and fine ladies were invited to the show, were hospitably regaled, and were delighted by seeing the divers in their panoply descend into the river, and return laden with old iron and ship's tackle. There was a Greenland Fishing Company, which could not fail to drive the Dutch whalers and herring busses out of the Northern Ocean. There was a Tanning Company, which promised to furnish leather superior to the best that was brought from Turkey or Russia. There was a society which undertook the office of giving gentlemen a liberal education on low terms, and which assumed the sounding name of the Royal Academies Company. In a pompous advertisement it was announced that the directors of the Royal Academies Company had engaged the best masters in every branch of knowledge, and were about to issue twenty

The Origin of the National Debt

thousand tickets at twenty shillings each. There was to be a lottery: two thousand prizes were to be drawn: and the fortunate holders of the prizes were to be taught, at the charge of the Company, Latin, Greek, Hebrew, French, Spanish, conic sections, trigonometry, heraldry, japanning, fortification, book-keeping, and the art of playing the theorbo. Some of these companies took large mansions and printed their advertisements in gilded letters, Others, less ostentatious, were content with ink, and met at coffee-houses in the neighborhood of the Royal Exchange. Jonathan's and Garraway's were in a constant ferment with brokers, buyers, sellers, meetings of directors, meetings of proprietors. Time bargains soon came into fashion. Extensive combinations were formed, and monstrous fables were circulated, for the purpose of raising or depressing the price of shares. Our country witnessed for the first time those phenomena with which a long experience has made us familiar. A mania of which the symptoms were essentially the same with those of the mania of 1720, of the mania of 1825, of the mania of 1845, seized the public mind. An impatience to be rich, a contempt for those slow but sure gains which are the proper reward of industry, patience, and

The Origin of the National Debt

thrift, spread through society. The spirit of the cogging dicers of Whitefriars took possession of the grave Senators of the City, Wardens of Trades, Deputies, Aldermen. It was much easier and much more lucrative to put forth a lying prospectus announcing a new stock, to persuade ignorant people that the dividends could not fall short of twenty per cent, and to part with five thousand pounds of this imaginary wealth for ten thousand solid guineas, than to load a ship with a well chosen cargo for Virginia or the Levant. Every day some new bubble was puffed into existence, rose buoyant, shone bright, burst, and was forgotten.*

The new form which covetousness had taken furnished the comic poets and satirists

---

* For this account of the origin of stockjobbing in the City of London I am chiefly indebted to a most curious periodical paper, entitled, " Collection for the Improvement of Husbandry and Trade, by J. Houghton, F. R. S." It is in fact a weekly history of the commerical speculations of that time. I have looked through the files of several years. In No. 33, March 17, 1692-3, Houghton says, " The buying and selling of Actions is one of the great trades now on foot. I find a great many do not understand the affair." On June 13, and June 22, 1694, he traces the whole progress of stockjobbing. On July 13, of the same year he makes the first mention of time bargains. Whoever is desirous to know more about the companies mentioned in the text may consult Houghton's Collection, and a pamphlet entitled Angliæ Tutamen, published in 1695.

The Origin of the National Debt

with an excellent subject ; nor was that subject the less welcome to them because some of the most unscrupulous and most successful of the new race of gamesters were men in sad colored clothes and lank hair, men who called cards the Devil's books, men who thought it a sin and a scandal to win or lose twopence over a backgammon board. It was in the last drama of Shadwell that the hypocrisy and knavery of these speculators was, for the first time, exposed to public ridicule. He died in November, 1692, just before his Stockjobbers came on the stage ; and the epilogue was spoken by an actor dressed in deep mourning. The best scene is that in which four or five stern Nonconformists, clad in the full Puritan costume, after discussing the prospects of the Mousetrap Company and the Fleakilling Company, examine the question whether the Godly may lawfully hold stock in a Company for bringing over Chinese ropedancers. " Considerable men have shares," says one austere person in cropped hair and bands ; " but verily I question whether it be lawful or not. These doubts are removed by a stout old Roundhead colonel who had fought at Marston Moor, and who reminds his weaker brother that the saints need not themselves see the ropedancing, and

The Origin of the National Debt

that, in all probability, there will be no rope-dancing to see. "The thing," he says, "is like to take. The shares will sell well; and then we shall not care whether the dancers come over or no." It is important to observe that this scene was exhibited and applauded before one farthing of the national debt had been contracted. So ill informed were the numerous writers who, at a later period, ascribed to the national debt the existence of stockjobbing and of all the immoralities connected with stockjobbing. The truth is that society had, in the natural course of its growth, reached a point at which it was inevitable that there should be stockjobbing whether there were a national debt or not, and inevitable also that, if there were a long and costly war, there should be a national debt.

How indeed was it possible that a debt should not have been contracted, when one party was impelled by the strongest motives to borrow, and another was impelled by equally strong motives to lend? A moment had arrived at which the government found it impossible, without exciting the most formidable discontents, to raise by taxation the supplies necessary to defend the liberty and independence of the nation; and at that very moment, numerous capitalists were looking

The Origin of the National Debt

round them in vain for some good mode of investing their savings, and for want of such a mode, were keeping their wealth locked up, or were lavishing it on absurd projects. Riches sufficient to equip a navy which would sweep the German Ocean and the Altantic of French pivateers, riches sufficient to maintain an army which might retake Namur and avenge the disaster of Steinkirk, were lying idle, or were passing away from the owners into the hands of sharpers. A statesman might well think that some part of the wealth which was daily buried or squandered might, with advantage to the proprietor, to the taxpayer, and to the State, be attracted into the Treasury. Why meet the extraordinary charge of a year of war by seizing the chairs, the tables, the beds of hardworking families, by compelling one country gentleman to cut down his trees before they were ready for the axe, another to let the cottages on his land fall to ruin, a third to take away his hopeful son from the University, when Change Alley was swarming with people who did not know what to do with their money and who were pressing everybody to borrow it?

It was often asserted at a later period by Tories, who hated the national debt most of

The Origin of the National Debt

all things, and who hated Burnet most of all men, that Burnet was the person who first advised the government to contract a national debt. But this assertion is proved by no trustworthy evidence, and seems to be disproved by the Bishop's silence. Of all men he was the least likely to conceal the fact that an important fiscal revolution had been his work. Nor was the Board of Treasury at that time one which much needed, or was likely much to regard, the counsels of a divine. At that Board sate Godolphin, the most prudent and experienced, and Montague, the most daring and inventive of financiers. Neither of these eminent men could be ignorant that it had long been the practise of the neighboring states to spread over many years of peace the excessive taxation which was made necessary by one year of war. In Italy this practise had existed through several generations. France had, during the war which began in 1672 and ended in 1679, borrowed not less than thirty millions of our money. Sir William Temple, in his interesting work on the Batavian federation, had told his countrymen that, when he was ambassador at the Hague, the single province of Holland, then ruled by the frugal and prudent De Witt, owed about five millions sterling, for

The Origin of the National Debt

which interest at four per cent was always ready to the day, and that, when any part of the principal was paid off, the public creditor received his money with tears, well knowing that he could find no other investment equally secure. The wonder is not that England should have at length imitated the example both of her enemies and of her allies, but that the fourth year of her arduous and exhausting struggle against Lewis should have been drawing to a close before she resorted to an expedient so obvious.

On the fifteenth of December, 1692, the House of Commons resolved itself into a Committee of Ways and Means. Somers took the chair. Montague proposed to raise a million by way of loan: the proposition was approved; and it was ordered that a bill should be brought in. The details of the scheme were much discussed and modified; but the principle appears to have been popular with all parties. The moneyed men were glad to have a good opportunity of investing what they had hoarded. The landed men, hard pressed by the load of taxation; were ready to consent to anything for the sake of present ease. No member ventured to divide the House. On the twentieth of January the bill was read a third time, carried up to the Lords

The Origin of the National Debt

by Somers, and passed by them without any amendment.*

By this memorable law new duties were imposed on beer and other liquors. These duties were to be kept in the Exchequer separate from all other receipts, and were to form a fund on the credit of which a million was to be raised by life annuities. As the annuitants dropped off, their annuities were to be divided among the survivors, till the number of survivors was reduced to seven. After that time, whatever fell in was to go to the public. It was therefore certain that the eighteenth century would be far advanced before the debt would be finally extinguished; and, in fact, long after King George the Third was on the throne, a few aged men were receiving large incomes from the State, in return for a little money which had been advanced to King William on their account when they were children.† The rate of interest was to be ten per cent till the year 1700,

* Commons' Journals; Stat. 4 W. & M. c. 3.

† William Duncombe, whose name is well known to curious students of literary history, and who, in conjunction with his son John, translated Horace's works, died in 1769, having been seventy-seven years an annuitant under the Act of 1692. A hundred pounds had been subscribed in William Duncombe's name when he was three years old; and, for this small sum, he received thousands upon thousands. Literary Anecdotes of the Eighteenth Century, viii. 265.

The Origin of the National Debt

and after that year seven per cent. The advantages offered to the public creditor by this scheme may seem great, but were not more than sufficient to compensate him for the risk which he ran. It was not impossible that there might be a counter-revolution ; and it was certain that if there were a counter-revolution, those who had lent money to William would lose both interest and principal.

Such was the origin of that debt which has since become the greatest prodigy that ever perplexed the sagacity and confounded the pride of statesmen and philosophers. At every stage in the growth of that debt the nation has set up the same cry of anguish and despair. At every stage in the growth of that debt it has been seriously asserted by wise men that bankruptcy and ruin were at hand. Yet still the debt went on growing ; and still bankruptcy and ruin were as remote as ever. When the great contest with Lewis the Fourteenth was finally terminated by the Peace of Utrecht the nation owed about fifty millions ; and that debt was considered, not merely by the rude multitude, not merely by foxhunting squires and coffee-house orators, but by acute and profound thinkers, as an incumbrance which would permanently cripple the

The Origin of the National Debt

body politic. Nevertheless trade flourished: wealth increased ; the nation became richer, and richer. Then came the war of the Austrian Succession: and the debt rose to eighty millions. Pamphleteers, historians, and orators pronounced that now, at all events, our case was desperate.* Yet the signs of increasing prosperity, signs which could neither be counterfeited nor concealed, ought to have satisfied observant and reflecting men that a debt of eighty millions was less to the England which was governed by Pelham than a debt of fifty millions had been to the England which was governed by Oxford. Soon war again broke forth ; and under the energetic and prodigal administration of the first William Pitt, the debt rapidly swelled to a hundred and forty millions. As soon as the first intoxication of victory was over, men of theory and men of business almost unanimously pronounced that the fatal day had now really arrived. The only statesman, indeed, active or speculative, who was too wise to share in the

* Smollett's Complete History of England from the Descent of Julius Cæsar to the Treaty of Aix la Chapelle, 1748, containing the Transactions of one thousand eight hundred and three years, was published at this time. The work ends with a vehement philippic against the government; and that philippic ends with the tremendous words, " the national debt accumulated to the enormous sum of eighty millions sterling."

The Origin of the National Debt

general delusion, was Edmund Burke. David Hume, undoubtedly one of the most profound political economists of his time, declared that our madness had exceeded the madness of the Crusaders. Richard Cœur de Lion and Saint Lewis had gone in the face of arithmetical demonstration. It was impossible to prove by figures that the road to Paradise did not lie through the Holy Land : but it was possible to prove by figures that the road to national ruin was through the national debt. It was idle, however, now to talk about the road : we had done with the road : we had reached the goal : all was over : all the revenues of the island north of Trent and west of Reading were mortgaged. Better for us to have been conquered by Prussia or Austria, than to be saddled with the interest of a hundred and forty millions.* And yet this great philosopher—for such he was,—had only to open his eyes, and to see improvement all around him, cities increasing, cultivation extending, marts too small for the crowd of buyers and sellers, harbors insufficient to contain the shipping, artificial rivers joining the chief inland seats of industry to the chief seaports, streets better lighted,

---

* See a very remarkable note in Hume's History of England, Appendix III.

The Origin of the National Debt

houses better furnished, richer wares exposed to sale in statelier shops, swifter carriages rolling along smoother roads. He had, indeed, only to compare the Edinburgh of his boyhood with the Edinburgh of his old age. His prediction remains to posterity, a memorable instance of the weakness from which the strongest minds are not exempt. Adam Smith saw a little, and but a little further. He admitted that, immense as the pressure was, the nation did actually sustain it and thrive under it in a way which nobody could have foreseen. But he warned his countrymen not to repeat so hazardous an experiment. The limit had been reached. Even a small increase might be fatal.* Not less gloomy was the view which George Grenville, a minister eminently diligent and practical, took of our financial situation. The nation must, he conceived, sink under a debt of a hundred and forty millions, unless a portion of the load were borne by the American colonies. The attempt to lay a portion of the load on the American colonies produced another war. That war left us with an additional hundred millions of debt, and without the colonies whose help had been represented as indispensable. Again England was given over;

* Wealth of Nations, book v. Chap. iii.

The Origin of the National Debt

and again the strange patient persisted in becoming stronger and more blooming in spite of all the diagnostics and prognostics of State physicians. As she had been visibly more prosperous with a debt of one hundred and forty millions than with a debt of fifty millions, so she was visibly more prosperous with a debt of two hundred and forty millions than with a debt of one hundred and forty millions. Soon however the wars which sprang from the French Revolution, and which far exceeded in cost any that the world had ever seen, tasked the powers of public credit to the utmost. When the world was again at rest the funded debt of England amounted to eight hundred millions. If the most enlightened man had been told, in 1792, that, in 1815, the interest on eight hundred millions would be duly paid to the day at the Bank, he would have been as hard of belief as if he had been told that the government would be in possession of the lamp of Aladdin or of the purse of Fortunatus. It was in truth a gigantic, a fabulous, debt; and we can hardly wonder that the cry of despair should have been louder than ever. But again that cry was found to have been as unreasonable as ever. After a few years of exhaustion, England recovered herself. Yet

The Origin of the National Debt

like Addison's valetudinarian, who continued to whimper that he was dying of consumption till he became so fat that he was shamed into silence, she went on complaining that she was sunk in poverty till her wealth showed itself by tokens which made her complaints ridiculous. The beggared, the bankrupt, society not only proved able to meet all its obligations, but while meeting those obligations, grew richer and richer so fast that the growth could almost be discerned by the eye. In every county, we saw wastes recently turned into gardens : in every city, we saw new streets, and squares, and markets, more brilliant lamps, more abundant supplies of water: in the suburbs of every great seat of industry, we saw villas multiplying fast, each embosomed in its gay little paradise of lilacs and roses. While shallow politicians were repeating that the energies of the people were borne down by the weight of the public burdens, the first journey was performed by steam on a railway. Soon the island was intersected by railways. A sum exceeding the whole amount of the national debt at the end of the American war was, in a few years, voluntarily expended by this ruined people on viaducts, tunnels, embankments, bridges, stations, engines. Meanwhile tax-

The Origin of the National Debt

ation was almost constantly becoming lighter and lighter: yet still the Exchequer was full. It may be now affirmed without fear of contradiction that we find it as easy to pay the interest of eight hundred millions as our ancestors found it, a century ago, to pay the interest of eighty millions.

It can hardly be doubted that there must have been some great fallacy in the notions of those who uttered and of those who believed that long succession of confident predictions, so signally falsified by a long succession of indisputable facts. To point out that fallacy is the office rather of the political economist than of the historian. Here it is sufficient to say that the prophets of evil were under a double delusion. They erroneously imagined that there was an exact analogy between the case of an individual who is in debt to another individual and the case of a society which is in debt to a part of itself; and this analogy led them into endless mistakes about the effect of the system of funding. They were under an error not less serious touching the resources of the country. They made no allowance for the effect produced by the incessant progress of every experimental science, and by the incessant effort of every man to get on in life. They

The Origin of the National Debt

saw that the debt grew: and they forgot that other things grew as well as the debt.

A long experience justifies us in believing that England may, in the twentieth century, be better able to pay a debt of sixteen hundred millions than she is at the present time to bear her present load. But be this as it may, those who so confidently predicted that she must sink, first under a debt of fifty millions, then under a debt of eighty millions, then under a debt of a hundred and forty millions, then under a debt of two hundred and forty millions, and lastly under a debt of eight hundred millions, were beyond all doubt under a twofold mistake. They greatly overrated the pressure of the burden: they greatly underrated the strength by which the burden was to be borne.*

---

*I have said that Burke alone among his contemporaries was superior to the vulgar error in which men so eminent as David Hume and Adam Smith shared. I will quote, in illustration of my meaning, a few weighty words from the Observations on the Late State of the Nation written by Burke in 1769. "An enlightened reader laughs at the inconsistent chimera of our author (George Grenville), of a people universally luxurious, and at the same time oppressed with taxes and declining in trade. For my part, I cannot look on these duties as the author does. He sees nothing but the burden. I can perceive the burden as well as he: but I cannot avoid contemplating also the strength that supports it. From thence I draw the most comfortable assurances of the future vigor and the ample resources of this great misrepresented country."

www.ingramcontent.com/pod-product-compliance
Lightning Source LLC
Chambersburg PA
CBHW020856230426
43666CB00008B/1209